soho
theatre company

Soho Theatre Company presents

BADNUFF

by **Richard Davidson**

First performed at Soho Theatre on 18 March 2004

Performances in the Lorenz Auditorium

Soho Theatre is supported by

Bloomberg   gettyimages

Registered Charity No: 267234

Soho Theatre Company has the support of the Pearson Playwrights' Scheme sponsored by The Peggy Ramsay Foundation.

Soho Theatre Company productions are supported by the Garfield Weston Foundation.

BADNUFF
by **Richard Davidson**

Brendan	Josef Altin
Jay	Rachel Harvey
Lanny	Michael Obiora
Maggie	Raquel Cassidy
Patsy	Petra Letang
Tom	David Harewood

Director	Jonathan Lloyd
Designer	Liz Cooke
Lighting Designer	Johanna Town
Sound Designer	Matt McKenzie
Fight Director	Paul Benzing
Casting	Ginny Schiller
Assistant Director	Sarah O'Gorman

Production Manager	Nick Ferguson
Stage Manager	Andrea Gray
Deputy Stage Manager	Laura Routledge
Assistant Stage Manager	Geraldine Mullins
Chief Technician	Nick Blount
Chief Electrician	Christoph Wagner
Lighting Technician	Ade Peterkin
Scenery built and painted by	Robert Knight Ltd.

Soho Theatre Company would like to thank:
Westminster Kingsway College, Blackheath High School

Press Representation: Nancy Poole (020 7478 0142)
Graphic Design: Jane Harper
Production photography: Sheila Burnett
Advertising: MandH Communications Ltd.

Soho Theatre and Writers' Centre
21 Dean Street
London W1D 3NE
Admin: 020 7287 5060
Fax: 020 7287 5061
Box Office: 020 7478 0100
www.sohotheatre.com
email: box@sohotheatre.com

THE COMPANY

Cast

Josef Altin Brendan

Josef's theatre credits include *Credible Witness* (Royal Court) and *Bugsy Malone* (National Youth Music Theatre at Queens Theatre, West End). Television credits include *Babyfather* (BBC). Film credits include *Dirty Pretty Things* (directed by Stephen Frears); *My Other Wheelchair is a Porsche* (Ravi Kumar) and *Esther Khan* (Magic Lantern Films).

Raquel Cassidy Maggie

Raquel's theatre credits include *Sunday Father* (Hampstead Theatre); *The Flu Season* (Gate Theatre); *Possible Worlds* (Tron Theatre); *Tree Houses* (Northcott Theatre, Exeter); *Blessings* (Old Red Lion); *The Promise* (Everyman, Liverpool); *Dogs Barking* (The Bush Theatre); *Threesome* (LPB Productions, Old Red Lion); *Othello* (Bury St Edmunds); *The Bone Room* (Young Vic Studio); *Twelfth Night* (Royal National Theatre); *The Censor* (Royal Court); *Couch Crass and Ribbon* (Watermill, Newbury); *Stealing Souls* (The Red Room); *Walking with Mr Brownstone* (Southwark Playhouse); *The Song from the Sea* (West Yorkshire Playhouse) and *St James and The Tattoo Man* (London New Play Festival). Television credits include *The Worst Week of my Life*, *Trevor's World of Sport* (Hat Trick Productions); *Thin Ice, Nature Boy* (BBC); *Killer Net* (Lynda La Plante) and *Teachers* (series 1 and 2, Tiger Aspect/Channel 4). Film credits include *Do I Love you?* (Best Feature, audience award at Cineffable Festival, Paris).

Rachel Harvey Jay

Rachel trained at the Sylvia Young Theatre School. Her appearance in *Badnuff* for Soho Theatre Company marks her London theatre debut. Theatre credits include *Romeo and Juliet* (Dustin Studios, Northants); *Road, The Wizard of Oz* (Derngate, Northants) and *He Who Says Yes, He Who Says No* (The Castle Arts Centre, Wellingborough). Television credits include *My Family* and *Victoria Wood* (BBC). Rachel also sings lead vocal in the band, *Corby*.

David Harewood Tom

David's theatre credits include *Antony and Cleopatra* (Public Theatre, New York and Riverside Studios, London); *Othello* (Royal National Theatre); *Peribanez* (Young Vic); *Mark Antony* (Alley Theatre, Houston); *Black Poppies, World's Apart*

(Stratford East); *Entertaining Mr Sloane* (Derby Playhouse); *King* (Piccadilly Theatre); *King Lear* (Talawa Theatre Co.); *One Over the Eight* (Stephen Joseph Theatre). Television credits include *The Vice* (Carlton Television); *Babyfather*, *For the Greater Good*, *Black Poppies*, *Agony Too* (BBC); *Fat Friends* (ITV); *Always and Everyone* (Granada Television) and *The Bill* (ITV). Film credits include *Away Through the Woods* (directed by Julian Fellows) and *The Merchant of Venice* (directed by Michael Radford).

Petra Letang Patsy

Petra's theatre credits include *Cameron's St* (Polka Theatre); *Fallout , Rampage, Breath Boom, Rough Road to Survival* (Royal Court); *Beautiful Thing* (Nottingham Playhouse, tour) *Local Boys* (Hampstead Theatre) and *Generations of the Dead* (Young Vic). Television credits include *Jonathan Creek*, *Babyfather* (BBC); *Wonderous Oblivion* (APT Film Ltd) and *Family Affairs* (Channel 5). Radio credits include *Ilford-Romford and All Stations*, *Miss Butterfly*, *The Silence of the Stars* and *Telltale* (BBC).

Michael Osbiora Lanny

Michael's theatre credits include *Fallout* (Royal Court); *Headstone* (Arcola Theatre) and *Exclude Me* (Chelsea Theatre). Television credits include *Powers*, *Holby City*, *Doctors*, *Grange Hill* (1996–2001), *My Family*, *Sea of Souls* (BBC); *Dogma: Take My Heart* (Channel 4) and *The Bill* (ITV).

Company

Liz Cooke Designer

Theatre work includes *Round the Horne* (West End); *Thyestes* (RSC); *The Recruiting Officer, Resurrection* (Lichfield Garrick); *Mother Courage* (Graeae tour); *Blue* (Old Vic);*The Accrington Pals* (West Yorkshire Playhouse); *The Birds* (National Theatre); *Notes From the Edge* (Belfast Festival and Huddersfield Music Festival);*The Split* (Strausser Productions); *Green Field* (Traverse); *And All the Children Cried* (West Yorkshire Playhouse and New End Hampstead); *The Magic Toyshop* (Shared Experience); *Destination* (Volcano); *Les Blancs* (Royal Exchange Theatre); *The Hackney Office* and *The Spirit of Annie Ross* (Druid Theatre); *Behsharam* (Soho Theatre, Birmingham Rep); *Spoonface Steinberg* (New Ambassadors, Kennedy Centre Washington); *The Daughter-in-Law, The Guests, Goodbye Kiss* (Orange Tree Theatre); *The Beauty Queen of Leenane* (Salisbury Playhouse); *The Gift* (Tricycle Theatre, Birmingham Rep); *The Glory of Living, Exposure* (Royal Court Upstairs); *Better* (BAC); *The Comedy of Errors* (Globe); *Cooking with Elvis* (Live Theatre, Whitehall); *The Idiot* (West Yorkshire Playhouse, tour) and *Volunteers* (Gate Theatre). Opera includes: *La Traviata, Don Giovanni* and *Carmen* (Holland Park Festival).

Richard Davidson Writer

Richard's first play, *Storybook*, premiered at the Edinburgh Fringe Festival where it won a Fringe First and was nominated for The Independent Theatre Award. Subsequent plays include *Conventional Demons* (The Pleasance, Edinburgh); *The Glass Ceiling* (BAC) and *Grey Matter* (Paines Plough at Bristol Old Vic, tour). After several years teaching, Richard now tutors students from across the country using video-conferencing technology. He also writes for *EastEnders.*

Jonathan Lloyd Director

Jonathan is Acting Artistic Director at Soho Theatre where he has directed *Mr Nobody, Modern Dance for Beginners, Julie Burchill is Away, School Play, Jump Mr Malinoff, Jump, The Backroom, Skeleton* and the Under-11s Playwriting Scheme. Other productions include *The Backroom* (Bush Theatre); *Perpetua* (Birmingham Rep); *Summer Begins* (RNT Studio, Donmar); *Channel Four Sitcom Festival* (Riverside Studios); *Serving It Up* (Bush); *Blood Knot* (Gate Theatre) and *Function of the Orgasm* (Finborough). As a writer for children's television: *Dog and Duck* (ITV) and *You Do Too* (Nickelodeon).

Matt McKenzie Sound Designer

Matt McKenzie came to the UK from New Zealand in 1978. He toured with Paines Plough before joining the staff at The Lyric Theatre Hammersmith in 1979 where he designed the sound for several productions. Since joining Autograph in 1984, Matt has been responsible for the sound design for the opening of Soho Theatre; *Vertigo* (Guildford); *Saturday, Sunday, Monday, Easy Virtue* (Chichester); *Frame 312* (Donmar); *Iron* (The Traverse and Royal Court). In the West End, theatre credits include *Made in Bangkok*, *The House of Bernarda Alba*, *A Piece of My Mind*, *Journey's End*, *A Madhouse in Goa*, *Barnaby and the Old Boys*, *Irma Vep*, *Gasping*, *Map of the Heart*, *Tango Argentino*, *When She Danced*, *Misery*, *Murder is Easy*, *The Odd Couple*, *Pygmailion*, *Things We Do for Love*, *Long Day's Journey into Night* and *Macbeth*. For Sir Peter Hall credits include *Lysistrata*, *The Master Builder*, *School for Wives*, *Mind Millie for Me*, *A Streetcar Named Desire*, *Three of a Kind* and *Amedeus* (West End and Broadway). Matt was Sound Supervisor for the Peter Hall Season (Old Vic and The Piccadilly) and designed the sound for *Waste*, *Cloud 9*, *The Seagull*, *The Provok'd Wife*, *King Lear*, *The Misanthrope*, *Major Barbara*, *Filumena* and *Kafka's Dick*. Work for the RSC includes *Family Reunion*, *Henry V*, *The Duchess of Malfi*, *Hamlet*, *The Lieutenant of Inishmore*, *Julius Ceasar* and *A Midsummer Night's Dream*.

Sarah O'Gorman Assistant Director

Sarah is a Television Director, working mainly for the BBC. This is her second theatrical production – Sarah was also Assistant Director on *Mr Nobody* at Soho Theatre.

Johanna Town Lighting Designer

Johanna has been Head of Lighting at the Royal Court since 1990 where recent lighting designs include *Food Chain*, *Under the Whaleback*, *Terrorism*, *Plastercine* and *Where Do We Live*. Her freelance lighting designs includes A *Permanent Way*, *She Stoops to Conquer, A Laughing Matter* (Out Of Joint / RNT); *The Steward of Christendom* (Out of Joint & Broadway); *Shopping & Fucking* (Out of Joint and West End); *I.D.* (Almeida); *The Dumb Waiter* (Oxford Playhouse); *Brassed Off* (Liverpool Playhouse, Birmingham Rep); *Justifying War* (Tricycle); *A Doll's House* (Southwark); *Feelgood* and *Little Malcolm & His Struggle Against the Eunuchs* (both Hampstead and West End); *Rose* (RNT / Broadway); *Top Girls* (West End); *Arabian Nights* and *Our Lady of Sligo* (both New York); *Ghosts* (Royal Exchange). She was last at Soho Theatre on *Mr Nobody.*

● soho
● theatre company

Soho Theatre Company is passionate in its commitment to new writing, producing a year-round programme of bold, original and accessible new plays – many of them from first-time playwrights.

'a foundry for new talent... one of the country's leading producer's of new writing' Evening Standard

Soho Theatre + Writers' Centre offers an invaluable resource to emerging playwrights. Our training and outreach pro-gramme includes the innovative Under 11's scheme, the Young Writers Group (15-25's) and a burgeoning series of Nuts and Bolts writing workshops designed to equip new writers with the basic tools of playwrighting. We offer the nation's only unsolicited script-reading service, reporting on over 2,000 plays per year. We aim to develop and showcase the most promising new work through the national Verity Bargate Award, the Launch Pad scheme and the Writers' Attachment Programme, working to develop writers not just in theatre but also for theatre, TV and film.

'a creative hotbed... not only the making of theatre but the cradle for new screenplay and television scripts' The Times

Contemporary, comfortable, air-conditioned and accessible, the Soho Theatre is busy from early morning to late at night. Alongside the production of new plays, it is also an intimate venue to see national and international comedians in an eclectic programme mixing emerging new talent with established names. Soho Theatre is home to Café Lazeez, serving delicious Indian fusion dishes downstairs with a lively bar upstairs that has a 1am licence.

'London's coolest theatre by a mile' Midweek

Soho Theatre Company is developing its work outside of the building, producing in Edinburgh and on tour in the UK whilst expanding the scope of its work with writers. It hosts the annual Soho Writers' Festival which brings together innovative practitioners from the creative industries with writers working in theatre, film, TV, radio, literature and poetry. Our programme aims to challenge, entertain and inspire writers and audiences from all backgrounds.

● soho
● theatre company

Soho Theatre and Writers' Centre
21 Dean Street, London W1D 3NE
Admin: 020 7287 5060 Fax: 020 7287 5061
Box Office: 020 7478 0100 Minicom: 020 7478 0136
www.sohotheatre.com   email: box@sohotheatre.com

Bars and Restaurant
Café Lazeez brasserie serves Indian-fusion dishes until 12pm.
Late bar open until 1am. The Terrace Bar serves a range of
soft and alcoholic drinks.

Email information list
For regular programme updates and offers, join our free email
information list by emailing box@sohotheatre.com or visiting
www.sohotheatre.com/mailing.

If you would like to make any comments about any of the
productions seen at Soho Theatre, why not visit our chatroom
at www.sohotheatre.com?

Hiring the theatre
Soho Theatre has a range of rooms and spaces for hire.
Please contact the theatre managers on 020 7287 5060, email
hires@sohotheatre.com or go to www.sohotheatre.com for
further details.

● soho
● theatre company

Artistic Director: Abigail Morris
Acting Artistic Director: Jonathan Lloyd
Assistant to Artistic Director: Nadine Hoare
Administrative Producer: Mark Godfrey
Assistant to Administrative Producer: Tim Whitehead
Writers' Centre Director: Nina Steiger
Literary Assistant: David Lane
Casting Director: Ginny Schiller
Marketing and Development Director: Zoe Reed
Development Officer: Gayle Rogers
Marketing Officer: Jenni Wardle
Marketing and Development Assistant: Kelly Duffy
Press Officer: Nancy Poole (020 7478 0142)
General Manager: Catherine Thornborrow
Front of House and Building Manager: Julia Christie
Financial Controller: Kevin Dunn
Book Keeper: Elva Tehan
Box Office Manager: Kate Truefitt
Deputy Box Office Manager: Steve Lock
Box Office Assistants: Janice Draper, Jennie Fellows, Leah
Read, Will Sherriff Hammond, Harriet Spencer and Natalie Worrall
Duty Managers: Mike Owen, Rebecca Storey, Peter Youthed
and Miranda Yates

Front of House staff: Rachel Bavidge, Louise Beere, Helene Le Bohec, Sharon Degan, Matthew Halpin, Sioban Hyams, Grethe Jensen, Carole Menduni, Katherine Smith, Rachel Southern, Maya Symeou, Luke Tebbutt, Minho Twon, Annabel Wood and Jamie Zubairi
Production Manager: Nick Ferguson
Chief Technician: Nick Blount
Chief LX: Christoph Wagner
Lighting Technician: Ade Peterkin

Board of Directors (*) and Members of the Company: David Aukin – chair*, Nicholas Allott*, Lisa Bryer, Tony Buckley, Sophie Clarke-Jervoise, Cllr Robert Davis, Tony Elliott*, Barbara Follett MP*, Norma Heyman*, Bruce Hyman, Lynne Kirwin, Tony Marchant, Michael Naughton*, David Pelham*, Michael Pennington, Sue Robertson*, Philippe Sands, Eric H Senat*, Meera Syal, Marc Vlessing*, Zoë Wanamaker, Sir Douglas Wass, Richard Wilson OBE*, Roger Wingate*

Honorary Patrons: Bob Hoskins *president*, Peter Brook CBE, Simon Callow, Sir Richard Eyre

Development Committee: Bruce Hyman – *chair*, Nicholas Allott, David Aukin, Don Black OBE, David Day, Catherine Fehler, Nigel Gee, Madeleine Hamel, Marie Helvin, Norma Heyman, Cathy Ingram, Carol Jackson, Roger Jospé, Lise Mayer, Patricia McGowan, Michael Naughton, Jane O'Donald, Marc Sands, Philippe Sands, Barbara Stone, Des Violaris, Richard Wilson OBE, Jeremy Zimmerman

THE SOHO THEATRE DEVELOPMENT CAMPAIGN

Soho Theatre Company receives core funding from Arts Council England, London and Westminster City Council. In order to provide as diverse a programme as possible and expand our audience development and outreach work, we rely upon additional support from trusts, foundations, individuals and businesses.

All of our major sponsors share a common commitment to developing new areas of activity and encouraging creative partnerships between business and the arts.

We are immensely grateful for the invaluable support from our sponsors and donors and wish to thank them for their continued commitment.

Soho Theatre Company has launched a new Friends Scheme to support its work in developing new writers and reaching new audiences. To find out how to become a Friend of Soho Theatre and what you will receive in return, contact the development department on 020 7478 0111, email development@sohotheatre.com or visit www.sohotheatre.com

Author's Note

In a school of a thousand kids, there are maybe a dozen names that every teacher is familiar with. These names are bellowed down corridors and across playgrounds, they provoke volcanic eruptions in period 5 Geography and synchronised groans in staff meetings. These names belong to the naughty boys, the naughty girls.

One of these names found its way onto my class register. Dan was fourteen and illiterate, slight for his age with big brown eyes and a lolloping walk that made him seem oddly puppy-like. Dan smelt stale, his fingers were yellowed by roll-ups and he was clearly stoned out of his box most of the time.

Although not violent to others, Dan was prone to self-destruction with a peculiar penchant for jumping out of first floor windows. This inexplicable behaviour might explain why, from the moment I met him, I felt drawn into his story, so when, after a few months, Dan stopped showing up for my English lessons, I made some enquiries and found he'd been permanently excluded from school – something to do with car theft or drugs, car theft on drugs? – and sent to a Pupil Referral Unit in the centre of Bristol.

On entering Red Cross Street Referral Unit, I immediately hooked into the chaotic energy that coursed through the building. Dan wasn't at the PRU that day, but a host of gregarious villains were more than willing to act as guides. Liberated from their old school uniforms, the kids fizzed around, screeching and shouting and swearing. But surface chaos aside, they seemed to want to be there. After an hour, I knew I'd be writing about PRUs and exclusion. *Badnuff* is the result.

Acknowledgements

With thanks to the staff and students at St Matthias Park Pupil Referral Service, Bristol and St Georges Centre, Cheltenham.

BADNUFF

First published in this version in 2004 by Oberon Books Ltd.
(incorporating Absolute Classics)
521 Caledonian Road, London N7 9RH
Tel: 020 7607 3637 / Fax: 020 7607 3629

e-mail: oberon.books@btinternet.com
www.oberonbooks.com

A catalogue record for this book is available from the
British Library.

ISBN: 1 84002 434 8

Cover photo: Nick White / Getty Images

Printed in Great Britain by Antony Rowe Ltd, Chippenham.

for Kate with love

Characters

TOM MARSHALL
Head of St. Peter's. Married with kids. Looks after himself.
Somewhere in his forties.

MAGGIE BATES
Teaches English / Humanities. Unmarried. Early thirties.

JAY WALSH
Goth-styled. Jet black hair with a white streak.
Fifteen years old.

BRENDAN CASEY
Scrawny and ferret-faced. Unconvincing facial hair.
White. Fourteen years old.

ORLANDO 'LANNY' HAYES
Athletic. Coiled spring. Black. Fifteen years old.

PATSY STONE
Fifteen years of age, but looks much older thanks
to a mix of make-up and experience. Mixed race.

It is pithily said: Give a dog an ill name and hang him; and it
may be added 'if you give a man, or race of men, an ill name,
they are very likely to do something that deserves hanging'.

Sir Walter Scott

Even a child is known by his actions,
by whether his conduct is pure and right.

Proverbs 20:11

I had been rinsed out of a couple of local schools...
I'd been that kid in the corner of the classroom, the street
corner. I had my back against the wall.

Dizzee Rascal
The Observer, September 2003

Setting
St. Peter's Educational Centre is a fictional Pupil Referral Unit.
Specialising in EBD (Educational and Behavioural
Difficulties), it offers a full-time education to twenty-four
permanently excluded KS4 students. Five teachers are
employed to deliver a basic curriculum to small groups of
between four and six students.

1

A classroom. Bleached, but for a sign proclaiming 'Respect' in large red letters. A few desks. A door leading to an off-stage store cupboard. A second door and window upstage. JAY enters.

JAY: I step into the room.

Beat.

Three figures watch me – count them – one…two…three – their laser sights flickering across my chest. No cover. One of those deep-frozen moments. Everything slows to ghost-speed –

PATSY: You know where you are girl?

LANNY: This ain't no dream.

BRENDAN: We're the naughty boys, the naughty girls – naughty, naughty, naughty!

LANNY trains an imaginary handgun on JAY and pulls the trigger.

LANNY: Ka-boom.

JAY: Just melt away…

BRENDAN: Don't worry, you'll be alright with us.

LANNY: Could be worse.

BRENDAN: Could be next door with the bottom-feeders.

PATSY: The thick pricks.

LANNY: Smell bad.

BRENDAN: Chip fat charlies.

PATSY: But we…we are *fine*.

LANNY: Ain't that the whole truth and nothing but.

LANNY and PATSY high-five.

JAY: The girl's holding a baby. A plastic baby.

PATSY: You givin' me screws?

JAY: I'm staring. Caught. Too late.

PATSY: It ain't clever to be screwin' your betters like that bitch.

JAY: Weighs me up: I'm not a threat.

PATSY: They make me look after this. Asked me to give her a name. So I called her Victoria, innit. Have to write a diary…explain how I feel about her and shit.

BRENDAN: See Patsy stole a baby –

PATSY: *Borrowed* a baby.

LANNY: Took it to school, kept it in her bag –

BRENDAN: Naughty, naughty –

PATSY: Bad example for the other kiddiewinks.

LANNY: Patsy loves the babies, don't you girl?

PATSY: So they give me this so's I know about consequences and shit. First night she woke me up crying…six in the morning! Wrapped her up tight in a sheet and buried the bitch in my wardrobe. She look like a Mummy from the old-time films.

BRENDAN: Everybody loves the cutesy little babbys –

PATSY: If they knew what I done, they'd be like 'See, that's what happens. You wouldn't be able to cope.' And I'd nod my head.

BRENDAN: Paint some shame on that face girl.

PATSY: But thing is, I know this dolly ain't real so it don't matter what I do. I can call her my baby bitch…I can spit on her, yeah?

LANNY: Tie her up…

PATSY: Could.

LANNY: Use her belly for an ashtray.

PATSY: Could.

LANNY: Dance on her chest.

PATSY: Could.

LANNY: Throw her 'cross the room.

BRENDAN: *Touch*-down!

PATSY: And next morning I'll turn up and say it was difficult, and yeah, I've reconsidered my attitude. 'Course I'll take the condoms. Fuckyes, don't want to be any trouble. Then I'll go out and shout. 'Come on boys I want what you got – give me that babyjuice!'

LANNY: Olympic standard!

PATSY: See, I know the difference between skin and plastic. And I ain't dumb. I know when it counts to be nice. And when it don't.

LANNY: (*To JAY.*) See, that's a story. You not got a story then? Can't come in if you ain't got a story.

BRENDAN: Listen. They go like this –

LANNY: So I'm sat in the Headmaster's office and he says –

BRENDAN: (*Priest-like singsong.*) 'Lanny Hayes, you've been summoned to account for the sins that weigh heavy on your soul.'

PATSY: Do it proper Brendan.

BRENDAN: He's tall and thin. Pop eyes, dry skin. And all the hair that should have been on his head, that's bushing out his nose, like he's rammed a hamster up –

LANNY: Fuckin' with my story?

BRENDAN: (*Arch-villain.*) 'So Mr Hayes, we meet again.'

LANNY: (*To BRENDAN.*) You know about me and my anger management problems chief.

BRENDAN: 'I understand you've been fighting again Lanny.'

LANNY: Weren't no fight.

BRENDAN: 'That's not what Miss Isaacs says.' The Head raises one eyebrow. Very cool party trick.

LANNY: A *fight* is a dispute between near equals –

PATSY: You said that?

LANNY: Yeah.

PATSY: You said dispute?

LANNY: Fuck off Pats.

BRENDAN: 'So how would you describe the *al-ter-cat-ion?*' Check *that* out.

LANNY: A massacre. I fuckin' killed the cunt.

BRENDAN: 'I'm shocked by your language. And now to guarantee me a good kicking….' (*Switching to terrace-style.*) 'Your big fat mama gone down on a Gooner!'

LANNY: So I kick shit out of the Head big-time. Pick up the Inter-Schools Netball Trophy. Bam! Lip bursts open. Slam! Head hits desk. Wham! Kick him in the Jacksons. Three-nil! He's fucked.

PATSY: In comes the secretary.

BRENDAN: Little Miss No-name.

PATSY: 'Call the police! Someone call the police!'

BRENDAN: Leaps over No-name like a Jedi knight.

LANNY: Race out of school.

PATSY: Down the river.

LANNY: Blaze some weed…

BRENDAN: (*PC Plod.*) 'Lanny Hayes. You are under arrest.'

LANNY: Going down in history.

PATSY: The school governors meet on a Wednesday night.

BRENDAN: 'Violent thug. Exclude the bastard. Permanently.'

LANNY: So here I am.

PATSY: So here we are.

BRENDAN: So what's *your* story?

JAY: They're looking at me.

BRENDAN: Done your homework have you?

PATSY: I'm a paranoid hysteric. S'true, look it up.

LANNY: Brendan's a dirty little tief.

BRENDAN: Half-inch your heart if you show me your jubblies – whereas Lanny here, he ain't interested, cos he's what's known as a repressed homosexual.

LANNY kicks out at BRENDAN but misses. BRENDAN darts away, keeping a desk between him and LANNY.

A psychopathic repressed homo. Resorts to violence when he ain't gettin' no arse-action. I've told him there are millions of men with the same *desires* – I just want him to be happy and free, take a trip into Soho, get down on one knee –

LANNY catches BRENDAN and throttles him over the desk. BRENDAN rolls out of LANNY's grip and darts over to the whiteboard and begins to sketch a woman with outsized breasts.

Me, I like the fairer sex. And the ladies, they love me right back. I'm talking *all night* –

PATSY: (*Scoffing at BRENDAN's picture.*) You never seen a pair of tits boy?

BRENDAN: I seen *your* titties Pats.

PATSY: You dream.

BRENDAN: I got a photo.

PATSY: Bollocks.

BRENDAN: Off Billy.

PATSY: Billy ain't got no photo.

BRENDAN: Trevor Neal give it him.

PATSY shuts up. LANNY laughs. Pause.

PATSY: What you laughin' about? There ain't no pictures.

LANNY: And the moral of this story? Don't ever – not never – get pissed up and kinky with a crack-head.

PATSY turns to JAY, who is trying not to laugh.

PATSY: And you can shut the fuck up you lezzyfuckinkeenerbitchlicker. What you doin' here anyhow? Fuck off quicktime –

BRENDAN: Alright Patsy, I admit it was a joke. I never been offered pictures of you flashing your nips in the back of Trev Neal's Mazda. And, if I had, I'm sure it'd cost me more than five Benson.

BRENDAN ducks as PATSY throws the baby and it narrowly misses his head.

LANNY: So come on then, what's your story?

PATSY: They don't send you here if you don't have a story.

BRENDAN: She don't have to say if she don't want to.

PATSY: Yeah, she do.

LANNY: You ain't comin' in if you ain't got a story.

The children disappear. The classroom dissolves and becomes…

2

A garden. A swing falls framelessly from the sky. MAGGIE swings gently as TOM pushes her.

TOM: Would you care to go higher Miss Bates?

MAGGIE: Always. The question is, are you up to it Mr Marshall?

TOM: I think I could manage a foot.

TOM puts his back into a push.

MAGGIE: We should make more of this place.

TOM: Here?

MAGGIE: We could have a garden.

TOM: A garden?

MAGGIE: It's a potential garden, isn't it?

TOM: Like I'm a potential leader of the free world?

MAGGIE: Realistic expectations please, Mr Marshall.

TOM: Achievable targets Miss Bates.

MAGGIE: Why couldn't we do it? Buy a few plants and some of that portable grass –

TOM: Turf.

MAGGIE: Exactly.

TOM: So you'd be willing to get your hands dirty –

MAGGIE: I live in a top-floor flat Tom – the closest I get to gardening is killing a pot of basil every fortnight. You're the one with the green fingers –

TOM: Fine. So I do all the work. And where would I get the money to pay for this instant garden?

MAGGIE: From the value-added fund.

TOM: And what value would having a school garden add, apart from giving our students a peaceful place to smoke?

MAGGIE: What's wrong with that?

TOM: I need to justify it Maggie.

MAGGIE: Well, they'd be learning about plants and soil. And turf. You think they get that opportunity at home?

TOM: So we're improving their environment *and* teaching them a valuable life-skill.

MAGGIE: Exactly.

TOM: Which they'll never need to know.

MAGGIE: They don't *need* to know why Henry the Eighth had it in for all those monks, but you still teach them that.

TOM: You just want a pretty place to eat your breakfast.

MAGGIE: And improving the working environment for your staff is a bad thing how?

TOM: Okay, okay, I'll run up some figures.

MAGGIE: We're talking a few measly plants.

TOM: I still need to check out the cost –

MAGGIE: And it'd look good when the LEA come round this week.

TOM: Now hang on –

MAGGIE: Imagine the scene: the hard-faced inspectors trudge into St. Peter's expecting the worst and what do they find? A beautiful garden, flowers in bloom, students playing croquet on the crisp new grass –

TOM: They're more likely to be smoking it.

MAGGIE: Don't be so cynical. Liberate your inner child Mr Marshall.

TOM: If my inner child was anything like our kids, I'd have had it whipped out years ago.

MAGGIE: You are such a hard-ass.

TOM: A what?

MAGGIE: A hard-ass.

TOM: Fine.

MAGGIE: Fine.

TOM: So you want a garden?

MAGGIE: It'd be good for us all.

TOM: Right.

> *TOM stops the swing.*

MAGGIE: That time already?

TOM: Nearly.

> *TOM cuddles MAGGIE round the waist and gently places his head on her shoulder.*

Can I see you tonight?

MAGGIE: I might have plans.

TOM: Really?

MAGGIE: And that's so surprising? I thought you played badminton on Monday nights.

TOM: Hazel's sprained her ankle.

MAGGIE: Oh dear.

TOM: Tragic. So what about tonight?

MAGGIE: What about the garden?

JAY enters the garden.

TOM: I'll look into it.

MAGGIE: And I'll look into my plans for the evening.

TOM: I'm begging you.

MAGGIE hears JAY and stands up and TOM turns to her, immediately assuming a rather awkward teacherly demeanour.

Lost?

JAY: No.

TOM: Can I help you?

JAY: I don't know.

MAGGIE: Are you Jay?

MAGGIE approaches JAY.

JAY: Yeah.

MAGGIE: Sorry, I'd forgotten you were starting today. I'm Maggie.

MAGGIE holds out her hand, but JAY doesn't shake.

MAGGIE: You'll be in my group.

TOM: So this is Jay from St. Jude's?

JAY nods.

Never had anyone from there.

Awkward beat.

MAGGIE: Tom's the teacher in charge, like a Headmaster –

TOM: (*Deadpan.*) All the land you see before you, from the lamp-post in the East to the rubbish bins in the West, this is my domain. The kingdom of Tom. Got it?

JAY smiles unconvincingly.

MAGGIE: Mostly we ignore him. But if you have any problems you can come to us and we'll help you sort them out –

JAY: I won't.

MAGGIE: Won't what?

JAY: Have any problems.

MAGGIE: Well, that's good.

TOM: Your mum said you'd been out of school a while.

JAY: Six months.

TOM: Today might be a bit weird then.

JAY: Maybe.

TOM: Yeah, maybe. You're a bit early, so why don't you go in the main door, turn left and let Mary take some details off you.

JAY walks slowly out. They watch her go.

Miserable sod. What d'you reckon, depressive?

MAGGIE: First day at a unit, you expect her to be jumping for joy? Least she looks harmless enough.

TOM: Take it you haven't read her report.

MAGGIE: Did you give it me?

TOM: I put it in your pigeon hole…

MAGGIE's expression suggests she hasn't checked her pigeon hole for some time. TOM gives her a tepid chastising look.

TOM: Assaulted a member of staff. Her mother's at the end of her tether, poor bitch. Tried to get her into every school north of the river, but she kept sabotaging her own interviews so now she's punishing herself by falling as far as she can for as long as she can –

MAGGIE: And we're Ground Zero.

TOM: Be lions and Christians all over again if we're not careful.

MAGGIE: I'll keep an eye on her.

MAGGIE starts to walk away.

TOM: See me tonight?

MAGGIE: In your dreams Mr Marshall.

MAGGIE walks off. TOM sits on the swing, a fat grin on his face.

3

The classroom. BRENDAN sits alone, finger jammed up his nostril. He springs up as MAGGIE enters.

MAGGIE: Morning Brendan.

BRENDAN: You owe me five minutes hardcore education Maggot. I got here on time, adjusted my attitude, pumped up the old brain cells and there's me, burning for that learnin' with not a teacher in sight. You stroked me up and left me stiff as a fuckin' goalpost – I'm frothin' up bigtime.

MAGGIE: Lovely –

BRENDAN: Truth. I'm workin' up a good old length –

BRENDAN shuts up as JAY enters.

MAGGIE: Brendan, this is Jay. She's going to be in our group.

BRENDAN: What's your favourite type of food?

JAY: I don't know.

MAGGIE: Take a deep breath Brendan. Remember, what we talked about –

BRENDAN: Anyone ever told you, you look like that bird off the X-Men? Skunk hair. Tongues the ice-boy. Who's your favourite superhero?

JAY: I don't know.

BRENDAN: Wolverine, Batman, Daredevil, Hulk…

JAY: I don't know.

BRENDAN: Well you should. These things matter.

MAGGIE: Leave Jay alone. You can interrogate her when you know her better.

BRENDAN: That's the whole point! You're always bangin' on about social skills for fuck's sake!

MAGGIE: Try conversation.

JAY: I'm a vegetarian.

MAGGIE and BRENDAN are stumped.

So my favourite food is vegetarian food.

BRENDAN looks really interested.

BRENDAN: So that's like, what, vegetables and shit?

JAY: Yeah, mostly.

BRENDAN: Favourite vegetable?

JAY: Dunno. I like peas.

BRENDAN: Wise choice. Can't fuck up a pea.

BRENDAN pronounces the 'p' in pea with an accentuated push of his lips and toys with the word whilst watching JAY. Rather disconcerting. MAGGIE watches him, waiting for the inevitable strike. She waits and waits until…

So you never had a big sloppy piece of meat in your mouth – ?

MAGGIE: That's enough!

BRENDAN: (*Mock-shocked.*) What? What did I say?

MAGGIE: You know what –

BRENDAN: Just takin' an interest. Fuckin' A! My auntie knows a vegetarian. Got a brain tumour.

MAGGIE: Come and get your pill please.

BRENDAN: You'll let me do the reg?

MAGGIE: There are only four of you, I think I can remember –

BRENDAN runs to MAGGIE's shoulder as she unlocks a drawer in her desk.

BRENDAN: We need rules…firm boundaries. If we don't have a register we forget where we are, who we are…you got to remember we're not *right.*

MAGGIE: Brendan, you're too close, just change down a gear.

BRENDAN smiles exaggeratedly, backs off a pace and takes the pill that MAGGIE offers him.

BRENDAN: We got to take our vitamins if we want to grow up healthy and strong.

BRENDAN necks the pill and grabs the register.

Casey, Brendan. Yes, sir! Slapper-Stone, Patsy. Knocking off. Hayes, Lanny. Dead most likely. Or in bed or stoned or both. Walsh, Jay.

Pause. BRENDAN looks up at JAY, waiting for her response.

Walsh, Jay.

JAY: Yeah.

BRENDAN: Yes, *sir*. Didn't they have a register in your last school?

JAY: *Yes*, sir.

BRENDAN: Hear that? Hear the way I got what I needed by use of my voice? You need to be firm with us or we'll forget the rules. And that's what we need, rules, lots of them. You been far too easy on us. My advice for today is go in hard and tough, especially with Lanny. He needs plenty of firm boundaries. And Patsy, you should give her some shit too, she likes to be walloped now and again. Knows it does her good –

MAGGIE: Thank you Brendan.

BRENDAN: You know when you was off last week, we had this supply teacher come in. Now, she really could've used some advice.

MAGGIE: And I'm sure you gave it to her.

BRENDAN: She smelt of cats. I'm allergic see –

MAGGIE: I remember you saying.

BRENDAN: They have a very sticky odour cats. Hard to shift. This supply teacher was like fuckin' Catwoman. Except she didn't dress in black leather or have a whip or do flips and shit…not in here anyhow. What I'm saying is – that girl didn't half smell of pussy.

Pause. MAGGIE decides not to react. BRENDAN pushes it…

She had a very distinctive pussy odour.

Beat.

The pussy smell was so bad it made my eyes water and my nose run.

MAGGIE: I'm a one-dog woman, you know that –

BRENDAN: I didn't know you had a dog.

MAGGIE: Well now you do.

BRENDAN: I kicked a puppy once.

MAGGIE: Well done.

BRENDAN: Can I come round your house and see your dog?

MAGGIE: Maybe one day.

BRENDAN: You let Lanny round your house –

MAGGIE: That was a very unusual circumstance.

BRENDAN: Fuckin' A, *I'm* an unusual circumstance.

MAGGIE: You certainly are. Now, if you've finished showboating –

BRENDAN: Catwoman taught us how to stay afloat in quicksand and treat frostbite – not at the same time. Also, how to wrestle a crocodile. Basically, you go for the eyes and nose. Or if it's a land attack you jump on its back and press down on the neck. And even if you get a teensy little cut you got to see a doctor, cos their mouths are full of infectious wotsits –

MAGGIE: Pathogens.

BRENDAN: Yeah, that's right. They fuck you up.

MAGGIE: Very useful information.

BRENDAN: So?

MAGGIE: So what?

BRENDAN: Can I come round your house?

MAGGIE: No.

BRENDAN: You know how to beat up a shark?

MAGGIE: Thump its nose.

BRENDAN: Common mistake. You gotta go for the gills mate.

MAGGIE: I will.

BRENDAN: Can I come round your house?

MAGGIE: One day.

BRENDAN: When?

MAGGIE: Some day.

BRENDAN: Tonight?

MAGGIE: *Some* day.

BRENDAN turns away from MAGGIE. When he turns back his cock hangs out of his trousers. MAGGIE's head falls to the desk in embarrassment. JAY doesn't know where to look.

Put it away.

BRENDAN: When can I come?

MAGGIE: I'm not going to be blackmailed.

BRENDAN: When?

MAGGIE: Put – your – penis – away.

BRENDAN: I just wanna see your stuff.

MAGGIE puts her hand on the phone.

MAGGIE: I'll call Tom.

BRENDAN: Lanny said you made him hot chocolate.

MAGGIE picks up the receiver.

MAGGIE: I'm not joking Brendan.

BRENDAN: *I* like hot chocolate.

PATSY enters the classroom.

PATSY: Oh man, you got that ugly little thing out again? Teensy little match-stick. Tryin' to start a fire, innit. That is *so* fucked-up.

BRENDAN: I *am* in the room you know.

BRENDAN puts his cock away.

PATSY: You showin' off for the new girl Brendan?

MAGGIE: (*To JAY.*) He likes to give himself an airing from time to time. Attention seeking. Not nice, I know.

PATSY: Ha ha. Oh boy, when Lanny finds out you been wagglin' your bits in here – shit man, he almost killed you last time.

MAGGIE: Patsy, nobody else needs to know about this.

BRENDAN: Ooh, hear that? Secrets! I love secrets –

MAGGIE: The things that go on in this room *stay* in this room, remember?

PATSY: Bet new girl likes secrets don't you, eh?

BRENDAN: Leave her alone.

PATSY: You got a mouth, ain't ya?

MAGGIE: We give people a chance to settle in, remember?

Beat.

PATSY: She said you come from St. Jude's.

JAY nods.

PATSY: With the nuns and shit?

JAY: Some nuns, yeah.

PATSY: They all lezzers or what?

MAGGIE: Enough.

PATSY: Bitch'll be back at her school quicktime. She don't think she has to make friends here, I can tell.

JAY squirms uncomfortably as PATSY stands over her.

You think you're better? I can tell you think you're better.

JAY: (*Quietly.*) I don't think I'm better.

PATSY: You squeak then little mouse?

JAY: I don't *think* I'm better.

PATSY: What's that supposed to mean?

MAGGIE: Right, let's all calm down –

PATSY: Tell me in plain English, what-the-fuck-is-that-supposed-to-mean?

MAGGIE takes PATSY by the arm. She pulls it off.

Get your fuckin' hands off me!

Silence.

BRENDAN: I could get my dick out again if it'd lighten the mood.

LANNY enters.

MAGGIE: Glad you could make it Lanny.

LANNY: S'alright. What's this?

LANNY nods nonchalantly Jaywards.

MAGGIE: This is Jay. You remember I told you about her?

LANNY: Nah.

LANNY approaches JAY, fixes her with his eyes.

PATSY: She's a rug-muncher.

LANNY: Grow up Pats.

PATSY: Piss off Lanny.

LANNY stands a little too close to JAY.

LANNY: So what d'you do?

JAY: Do?

LANNY: To get kicked out.

JAY: That your business?

LANNY: Nah.

PATSY: She been getting nasty with nuns –

LANNY: What nuns?

MAGGIE: (*In.*) Enough now –

PATSY: At her old school.

LANNY: You went to a school for nuns?

JAY: *Run* by nuns –

LANNY: So *you* ain't a nun –

JAY: 'Course I'm not.

BRENDAN: A convent school, dipshit.

LANNY: What the fuck d'you know?

BRENDAN: I'm a quarter Irish.

LANNY: And three quarters twat. Congratulations –

MAGGIE: Lanny!

LANNY: Sorry. I'm backing down. See? I'm backing down.

MAGGIE: Jay can tell you all about herself in her own sweet time –

JAY: I pushed a teacher.

Beat.

PATSY: (*Unimpressed.*) Yeah? – and?

JAY: She fell down some steps.

PATSY: So?

JAY: Three broken ribs, two broken arms and a punctured lung –

LANNY: *Fuck* –

PATSY's wants to take the spotlight off JAY.

PATSY: We goin' on the computers or not?

MAGGIE: Not.

PATSY: Why?

MAGGIE: You're going to write me some coursework.

BRENDAN: Ha ha.

MAGGIE: The English Language syllabus demands that you do a little non-fiction writing. Anyone knows what fiction is?

BRENDAN: Patsy got friction burns on her ass.

PATSY: They was *carpet* burns dipshit.

BRENDAN: Bump and grind all night on the deep shag, am I right Pats?

MAGGIE: That's enough. We're talking about fiction, not friction.

BRENDAN: Alright. Friction is what you get when you shag Pats, *fiction* is when you say you enjoyed it.

MAGGIE: That's right.

PATSY: What?

MAGGIE: I mean the concept is right.

PATSY: Lanny, you goin' to let this slide?

LANNY: I ain't your fuckin' bodyguard.

PATSY: Brendan got his dick out before.

MAGGIE: Okay, okay. Calm. Can we please have a moment's calm?

Silence. Out of MAGGIE's view, BRENDAN thrusts his pelvis in PATSY's direction.

PATSY: Tosser!

PATSY kicks her desk over. MAGGIE whips round to BRENDAN who beams angelically.

MAGGIE: Fiction. Non-fiction.

LANNY: Nuff with this teacher stuff. Just tell us the answer.

JAY: Fiction's stuff that's made up. Like stories.

They all turn to face JAY. She carries on regardless.

Fairytales and detective books, they're fiction. Romantic stories and Shakespeare and stuff. Non-fiction's all the stuff that isn't made up. Newspapers and diaries and food labels and –

PATSY: Fuckin' hell.

MAGGIE: Patsy!

PATSY: Don't shout at me!

MAGGIE: I'm sorry, sorry. Jay, that was great. Did you all get that? Fiction's stuff that's made-up. Non-fiction isn't. So, bearing that in mind, if you were going to write an autobiography would that be fiction or non?

Pause.

Autobiography.

No response.

You heard of that word Brendan? Lanny?

PATSY: Fuck me Maggs. Ain't *you* learned nothing?

MAGGIE: I'm sorry?

PATSY: All these questions and shit. Jus' give us a map to colour.

MAGGIE: We're not looking at maps.

PATSY: If you didn't have these inspectors coming round, you'd let us.

MAGGIE: That's not true.

PATSY: We ain't been on the computers this week.

MAGGIE: And you won't be.

PATSY: Fuck this shit –

MAGGIE: Sorry?

PATSY: I *said* –

JAY: It's a kind of story – a story of someone's life.

MAGGIE: That's right. Exactly.

PATSY: Keener bitch.

MAGGIE: A story of someone's life. That's the biography bit. What about the 'auto' part? Think of some other words that begin with auto. Lanny?

Pause. LANNY just stares.

BRENDAN: Automatic.

PATSY: Autoshutthefuckup –

JAY: Autopilot.

BRENDAN: Automobile.

MAGGIE: Good. That's good. Before automobiles, people couldn't drive themselves around. They could be *mobile*, but someone else was always doing the driving. So what d'you think *auto* means when you stick it on the front of a word? How does it change that word?

BRENDAN: It's do it yourself, innit.

MAGGIE: Excellent Brendan.

BRENDAN: S'like autoeroticism. When you fuck yourself.

Beat.

MAGGIE: Yep, same rule applies.

BRENDAN: All them geezers with fruit in their mouth and bags over their heads so's they can't breathe proper. Half-hangin' themselves and shit so's they get a bigger stiffy –

MAGGIE: Brendan –

BRENDAN: I seen it in a magazine, this geezer he's got a black mask on and this strap round his face with this thing like an egg – only bigger – stuffed in his mouth. He's got one hand on his old man and the other shoving some fruit up his ass – no, not fruit, vegetable – what d'you call that vegetable, like a courgette only bigger?

MAGGIE: Marrow?

BRENDAN: Yeah yeah, he's got a marrow up his ass.

PATSY: If he gets his dick out again, I fuckin' swear I'll rip it off.

BRENDAN: Not for the first time darlin' –

LANNY: Fuckin' take that back you pervy little cunt!

LANNY slaps BRENDAN full across the face. He could strike again when...

MAGGIE: Orlando!

PATSY laughs hysterically. JAY just sits, staring ahead.

MAGGIE: Jesus, Lanny.

PATSY gasps exaggeratedly.

PATSY: Language, Maggie.

MAGGIE: (*Smiling.*) Yeah well, that'll just have to be another one of our little secrets – like this – this disagreement. Brendan, you okay?

BRENDAN: Swallowed my gum.

PATSY: Shouldn't be chewing.

PATSY blows a large bubble.

MAGGIE: This doesn't have to go any further. Lanny, d'you want this to stop here in this room? You're already on a warning. If I have to send you to Tom again, I don't know what he'll do.

BRENDAN: You goin' to let him off?

MAGGIE: (*To LANNY.*) Remember what we talked about? You've got your appeal hearing tomorrow night. You want this to go further?

LANNY gives a faint shake of his head.

Alright then.

BRENDAN: What about me? What if I want it to go further?

MAGGIE: He only slapped you.

BRENDAN: He assaulted me. I want him to go see Tom.

MAGGIE: There's no need.

BRENDAN: Either he goes or I do.

MAGGIE: Fine. Lanny, go and sit outside Tom's office and wait for me.

MAGGIE: If he asks why you're there, tell him you're thinking about your autobiography. Biography – the story of someone's life. Auto – you do it yourself. Autobiography – the story of *your* life.

LANNY: I ain't got no fuckin' story.

MAGGIE: Oh yes you have. Now go and sit and think.

LANNY: Fine.

MAGGIE: Good. And don't slam the –

LANNY exits, slamming the door.

Door.

Beat.

PATSY: Oh boy, he's gonna fuck you up after-hours Brendan.

BRENDAN: Shakin' with fear.

PATSY: You *know* it's the truth.

BRENDAN: Your fault anyhow. Shouldn't be sendin' out all them sex vibes.

PATSY: Yeah, right.

BRENDAN: I'm sitting here trying to think about important stuff and you're zappin' me with lust rays – fillin' my fuckin' head with horniness. Juicin' me up when I'm tryin' to focus on my English. You gotta stop that shit.

PATSY: You hear this? This is what I'm on about. He's just wishfuckin' me.

BRENDAN: I'm undressin' you now Pats. In my mind I'm undressin' you.

PATSY: Wishfuckin' me. You hear this? Fuckin' peedowhatsit's wishfuckin' me.

BRENDAN: (*Eyes closed.*) Ride the pony Pats. Ride my fuckin' pony!

PATSY: Gonna cut your fuckin' ponydick right off!

BRENDAN: That's right. Throw me some more.

BRENDAN claps his hands and barks like a seal.

MAGGIE: Enough.

PATSY: Cunt don't even know when he's bein' dubbed.

BRENDAN: Rub-a-dub-dub! Patsy's in the tub, ridin' my big fat fuckin' pony –

MAGGIE: Enough!

The pair are jolted by the severity. Silence.

Take a step back and look at yourselves. Listen to yourselves. This isn't normal behaviour. You've got to realise that this is not the way normal people behave out there. Outside. In regular schools. In jobs. Most people can talk to each other. They can listen. And when they talk they don't litter their sentences with foulness.

Beat.

I've told you we can have secrets in here. What goes on in here, stays in here. But that gives me rights too. I've got the right to tell you the truth, and the truth is – your behaviour is not normal. You're here because you're not normal. Normal people don't kidnap babies and take them to school in their bags. Normal people don't wave their genitals around in lessons and spray obscene graffiti on the deputy head's car. These things are not normal.

BRENDAN: How are you defining 'normal'?

JAY: Shutupshutupshutupppp! SHUT UP!

Pause.

PATSY: (*Giggling.*) Jesus H!

BRENDAN: I'm sorry –

PATSY: You some kind of freak or what?

BRENDAN: Leave her alone.

PATSY: Whatsamatter Brendan, you eyein' up a nunfuck?

BRENDAN: I'm not eyein' up nothing.

MAGGIE approaches JAY who sits with her head on the desk.

MAGGIE: Are you alright?

JAY: (*Muffled.*) Yes.

A long pause. MAGGIE retreats and sits on her desk.

MAGGIE: Alright. Let's try and stick to the rules. For just one morning we'll try and go without swearing.

PATSY: What the fuck you on about?

BRENDAN: Like the Muslims goin' without food and shit.

MAGGIE: That's right.

BRENDAN: A fuck-fast.

MAGGIE: If you like. We'll start by clearing out our systems –

BRENDAN: Like colonic whatsit.

MAGGIE: Irrigation.

PATSY: What the fuck?

BRENDAN: S'when they stick a hoover up yer back
passage and suck out all the crap –

PATSY: Just like a normal hoover?

MAGGIE: No, a special hoover. Throw some words at me.
Angry words. Come on. Abuse me.

Pause.

JAY: Fucking cunt.

MAGGIE: Fucking and cunt. Old faithfuls.

BRENDAN: Tosser, wanker, shithead, arsewipe.

MAGGIE: Good, got anymore?

PATSY: Fuckface.

MAGGIE: More fucks?

BRENDAN: Fuckhead.

MAGGIE: Fuckbrain?

PATSY: Fuckbag.

BRENDAN: Fuck*pig.* Motherfucker.

PATSY: Arsefucker.

BRENDAN: Patsyfucker.

PATSY: Fuck off!

PATSY throws a book at BRENDAN.

BRENDAN: Fuckwit.

MAGGIE: Fuckstick.

BRENDAN: Fuckflaps.

PATSY: Fuck-me boots.

BRENDAN: (*Looking at PATSY.*) Fuck-me eyes.

MAGGIE: Fuck. This. For a game of soldiers. We're done.

BRENDAN: That was fuckin' A! Let's go again.

MAGGIE: That's it. They're gone. Don't want to hear them in this room again this morning.

PATSY: Yeah, *right.*

MAGGIE: I'm serious.

PATSY: Some teachers tried that before.

MAGGIE: And to make it a little more interesting we'll put some money on the line.

MAGGIE pulls out a handful of change and divides it into three small piles. The kids watch her, interested.

That's £1.90 each. My present to you. But every time you swear, I get twenty pence back.

PATSY: Shit man.

MAGGIE: I'll ignore that one.

PATSY: That ain't swearing.

MAGGIE hands each child a stack of the coins.

BRENDAN: Yeah it is, you muppet slag.

PATSY: You hear that?

MAGGIE: Yep. Shit and slag are both outlawed for the morning okay? We're going to try and be civil to each other.

PATSY: This ain't fair.

MAGGIE: Why not?

PATSY points at JAY.

PATSY: That freak don't say nothing anyhows.

BRENDAN: You can't call her that anymore.

PATSY: It ain't started yet. Bitch.

MAGGIE: Okay, okay. Starting from…now.

BRENDAN has taken a seat opposite PATSY. He stares at her fixedly.

Now I want you to start thinking about your autobiographies and, to help you do that, I've written out a few guidelines which I'd like you to keep in your English coursework folders –

PATSY: Stop lookin' at me Brendan.

MAGGIE: Jay, your school sent me your folder.

MAGGIE takes a folder from her desk…

I haven't had a chance to read it yet.

…and hands it to JAY.

PATSY: He's lookin' at me. Tell him to stop lookin'.

MAGGIE: Brendan would you please stop looking at Patsy.

PATSY throws a book at BRENDAN.

Don't throw please Patsy.

PATSY: Do your fucking job then and tell him to stop looking at me.

MAGGIE: Just ignore him.

BRENDAN: Twenty p-p-p-pee please P-P-P-Pats.

PATSY throws a coin at BRENDAN. It strikes him but he keeps staring at her.

MAGGIE: Jay, did you do any non-fiction coursework?

JAY: No.

PATSY: Take your fuckin' eyes off me –

BRENDAN: Twenny pee.

PATSY: You fucking disgusting little prick –

BRENDAN: Twenny pee… Forty pee.

PATSY: (*Turning to MAGGIE.*) Stop him looking at me.

PATSY seems genuinely upset now.

MAGGIE: Brendan, just calm down.

BRENDAN: I'm calm chief.

PATSY: (*Screaming.*) Get out you cunt!

BRENDAN: Twenny pee.

PATSY takes the handful of change, throws it at BRENDAN and darts out of the door. JAY's head falls to the desk, her arms wrapped round her ears. MAGGIE's gaze falls heavily on BRENDAN.

What? What did I do?

Lights snap off, and fade up on…

4

TOM's office. TOM and LANNY sit, a moody silence broken by…

TOM: Last night I was flicking through the dictionary. I like to learn a new word every day. One shiny new word. You ever heard this one? Nepenthes. Sounds like a flower doesn't it? One of those flowers that clings to the sides of old buildings. It's an old word. Greek. D'you know what it means?

LANNY: Do I look Greek to you?

TOM: Nepenthes. A drug causing the forgetfulness of sorrow.

LANNY: I ain't into drugs.

TOM: I know that.

LANNY: So what you on about?

TOM: It's an old word, sorrow, but I think you're full of it.

LANNY: I ain't full of nothing. I'm just me.

TOM: All that sorrow inside you, all that thick black engine oil, just waiting to spill out. Some people cry it out, but not you, no way. Cry? Lanny Hayes don't cry. But that black stuff, it's *got* to come out, hasn't it? So when someone flicks a switch – bang! – you're off , and that body of yours is like a magic engine turning sorrow into anger and kicking and screaming and slapping and biting –

LANNY: Brendan was winding me up.

TOM: My wife winds me up some days, my kids too, but I don't hit them.

LANNY: If I was back at my old school I wouldn't hit no-one.

TOM: For crying out loud Lanny, why d'you think they chucked you out?

LANNY: Things are different now.

TOM: By your own admission, you've just hit Brendan.

LANNY: I was provoked.

TOM: So come speak to me and *I'll* sort it out, yes?

LANNY: Yeah.

TOM: Maggie says you've got things under control and Maggie knows you best, so I'll go along with that. Says you're desperate to get back to Larkhill. You need GCSE Science to get to where you want to be. That right?

LANNY: Yeah. I want to do forensics. Like on the TV. D'you know what that is?

TOM: I do. I didn't know you were into science.

LANNY: Yeah, well I am now. And I've changed in other ways too. It's like I see things differently…the things I done before, I think about them and I don't feel good about it, you know? …Like at Larkhill we had this chemistry teacher called Ronson. Way little he was, with this floppy ginger hair. He'd be in the middle of a lesson and someone'd call him a bad name, and he'd be like – 'I don't know why you're *dissing* me' – you know, trying to use our words. At the end of every lesson, he'd stand by the door and try to touch fists with all the badboys, you know, 'Respect boys, respect'. Guy was a proper fool. Always wore the same blue tie and he got these marker stains on all his shirts where we'd sneaked up and drawn on him like he was nothing. He didn't stay long.

Beat.

I wish I hadn't done that now.

TOM: Well, you know we can't offer science here, so I'll speak for you at this appeal tomorrow night. But only on the condition that you cut out all this hard-man crap. Maggie thinks you're worth helping and it's taken her a lot of time and effort to get you this meeting, so I don't want you letting her down. Or me for that matter.

LANNY: I won't.

TOM: So tomorrow night, when we're all sat round the table, the Head and the Governors, the great and the good, what d'you think I should say about Lanny Hayes?

LANNY: I dunno.

TOM: No ideas?

LANNY: Maybe you could say I was doing better now.

TOM: And that you deserve a second chance?

LANNY: Yeah.

TOM: Then that's what I'll say.

LANNY: Thanks.

TOM: You keep out of trouble for the next couple of days or I might be changing my script – understand?

LANNY: Yeah.

LANNY gets up to leave.

TOM: And maybe you could make us all some of that nepenthes in your next chemistry class.

LANNY: Whatever Tom, whatever.

A knock at the door. MAGGIE pops her head round.

MAGGIE: Everything okay?

TOM: Fine. We've been having a little chat, but we're all done now.

MAGGIE comes in.

TOM: See you later Lanny.

LANNY: Later.

LANNY leaves. TOM waits for the door to close.

TOM: A forensic scientist! Did you put that idea in his head?

MAGGIE: No. He's seen some programme on TV.

TOM: And you didn't think to tell him about the problems he might encounter along the way –

MAGGIE: Even if he never makes it –

TOM snorts.

Even if he never makes it, his behaviour's improved, he's doing his work, he's got a target –

TOM: And when he falls short?

MAGGIE: You think he'll go off the rails and start jacking old ladies.

TOM: He's probably doing that already, only you're too starry-eyed to see it. Just take an honest look at him, at all of them –

MAGGIE: What are you going to say at his appeal tomorrow?

TOM: Marry me.

MAGGIE: Be sensible. Tomorrow. You. Lanny. Appeal.

TOM: Tomorrow? Tomorrow I'm going to lie through my teeth.

MAGGIE: It won't be lying if you say he's really trying to change.

TOM: To be honest, I don't think it'd make a blind bit of difference if I turn up or not.

MAGGIE: Of course it will.

TOM: The very fact that they've agreed to the meeting suggests they're ready to take him back. Larkhill are struggling to manage a fifty grand budget deficit, and Lanny's worth an extra six. So they take him back, stick him in some glorified cupboard they call an inclusion unit and skip off to the bank with a song in their heart.

MAGGIE: He's desperate Tom.

TOM: I know he is, but I also know he'd be best served here. Look, I've got Tweedledum and Tweedledee from the LEA gunning to close us down. So they show up on the very same day we push a prime head-banger back into mainstream. The gun's in my hand, I'm pointing it at my foot...

MAGGIE's unimpressed. TOM sees it.

Oh don't look at me like that.

MAGGIE: Take him seriously then.

TOM: I am. How's the new girl getting on?

MAGGIE: Patsy's marked out her territory and the boys have been indulging in a manic dick-swinging contest – quite literally in Brendan's case.

TOM throws MAGGIE a file.

TOM: Give this a read. It's Jay's account of what happened. It starts off 'the teacher slipped, not me guv' – and ends by saying she probably *was* to blame because she's an evil bitch and she hates the world and blah-di-blah-di-blah –

MAGGIE: (*Sarky.*) Sounds like a page-turner.

TOM: First impressions – think she's a nutter?

MAGGIE: What?

TOM: In your professional opinion would she benefit from sessions with the ed-psych?

MAGGIE: We've been together a morning Tom.

TOM: Sometimes a morning's enough. Look at Brendan. So stay alert out there and take care on the stairs.

MAGGIE: She seems like a nice girl.

TOM: I'm sure she is, but if you suspect she might be nice *and* nutty, let me know. Talking of nice girls. You. Me. Tonight. Chinese –

MAGGIE: I told you, I might have plans.

TOM: I've ordered plants for your garden.

MAGGIE: The *school*'s garden.

TOM: Pick you up at eight?

MAGGIE: I'm not sure I like you anymore.

TOM: Marry me.

MAGGIE: Slight problem there Tom –

TOM: I love you.

MAGGIE: And Hazel?

TOM: That was a low blow.

MAGGIE: I'll call you.

MAGGIE walks off. TOM sits and smiles. Lights down.

5

The front steps. PATSY sits cradling her fake baby. LANNY smokes a fag.

PATSY: After Jolene smashed that bottle, Ally tells us to get out the pub. Can't hardly blame him, but Sean tells him to fuck right off. So Ally reaches down under the bar and pulls out this crowbar, roars like Tarzan and chucks it straight at Sean's head. He ducks and it hits that blind geezer from the chippy. Ally pops up onto the bar like he's twenty-one again, and he's about to jump Sean slam-style when he slips on a beer-mat and skewers himself on the Fosters pump.

PATSY starts to laugh hysterically.

I don't ever want to hear someone scream like that again in this life –

But LANNY isn't laughing.

Why ain't you listenin' to me?

LANNY: I was thinking.

PATSY throws the baby to the floor.

PATSY: Since when you started thinking about stuff?

LANNY: Always have. But now I'm thinking about other stuff.

PATSY: So what you thinking about now?

LANNY: Dunno. New stuff.

PATSY: And what d'you used to think about?

LANNY: Different stuff.

PATSY: Fuck me Lanny, you should write a book.

LANNY smiles.

LANNY: The future. D'you ever think about that?

PATSY: Yeah, course.

LANNY: You know what you want and everything?

PATSY: I got it all planned out. First I'm gonna get a fella that cares about me and treats me nice. We'll get a little flat. Then we'll have a family. Two kids, maybe three. I'll go to college to do aromatherapy and then I'll set up my own business. Get a little car so I can visit rich people's houses and do my thing.

LANNY: What thing?

PATSY: I just said. Aromatherapy. Making people smell good.

LANNY: How d'you fix on that then?

PATSY: My auntie's into smells. She thieved all this stuff from Body Shop, like lavender oil and special soap made from seaweed and orange peel and shit. What about you?

LANNY: Dunno. Get back into Larkhill, hook up with my boys, kick-start another band, make some noise, make some moolah –

PATSY: If you get back into Larkhill, I'll still see you won't I?

LANNY: We live on the same estate don't we? Probably bump into you most weeks.

PATSY: You could take me out one night.

LANNY: (*Non-committal.*) If you like.

PATSY: Like you say, we'd prob'ly bump into each other.

LANNY flings a stone with a vicious whip of the arm.

Watch it Lanny. You'll hit the dog.

LANNY: Gives me the heebies, shufflin' round and round like that.

PATSY: No reason to throw stuff at it.

LANNY: Ain't it got no owner?

PATSY: That's the pub dog.

LANNY flings another stone. A yelp.

Now look what you've gone and done.

LANNY: It's only a dog.

PATSY: That's the second dog you nearly killed this week.

LANNY studies the offstage dog.

LANNY: Hey look at it now – gone all weird.

PATSY: It's bouncing.

LANNY: You're right. I ain't never seen a dog bounce like that before. We should make a tape – send it to the telly.

PATSY: You probably scizzed up its brain wiring. Dog wants to run away, brain tells its legs to bounce.

LANNY: Didn't hit its head.

PATSY: Don't have to. You probably hit a pressure point – like the Chinese use – you know, for acupuncture. Stick a needle in your leg and it relaxes your brain. Stick one in your arm and it makes you romantic.

LANNY: Like this?

LANNY holds PATSY's arm, pulls out a knife and makes stabbing gestures up and down. She pulls away.

PATSY: Get off!

LANNY: Easy Pats.

Beat.

PATSY: Where d'you get it?

LANNY: Some youts. It's the lick.

PATSY: What you need a knife for?

LANNY: Protection.

PATSY: From what?

LANNY: People.

PATSY: What people?

LANNY: Bad people, you get me?

LANNY sniffs her neck.

What's that smell?

PATSY: Ylang-ylang.

LANNY: You what?

PATSY: Ylang-ylang. My auntie give it me. Relaxes you. And it's an aphrodisiac.

LANNY: Like rhino horn innit.

PATSY: Comes from a plant Lanny.

LANNY: Gives you the horn without the rhino.

PATSY: You're a silly sod.

LANNY looks off.

LANNY: Wonder why someone don't look after that dog.

PATSY: Because it's ugly and it's fucked and you can't do anything with it.

The doll starts crying.

Bitch is pissing me off. I'm going down the shop. You want?

PATSY hands LANNY the doll.

LANNY: Monster Munch. Pickled onion.

PATSY exits. LANNY cradles the doll, gently rocking her. The crying subsides.

You just want your daddy, little girl? Ah, there-there. You just want your daddy.

LANNY rocks the baby gently as the lights fade down.

6

The classroom. BRENDAN stands at the whiteboard, mid-way through a game of hangman with a bored-looking JAY, who isn't paying him or the game much attention. The semi-completed title reads –'_ o_eo / and /_u_ _et'

BRENDAN: Come on, you got to pay attention.

JAY: I don't know many films.

BRENDAN: You'll definitely know this one.

JAY: P.

BRENDAN: No.

BRENDAN adds a line to the hangman drawing.

JAY: Z.

BRENDAN: You've done Z and I said no – and how many films got Z in the title anyhow?

JAY: Q.

BRENDAN: Q? Fuckin' Q? Nah, look at the board. It's easy.

JAY: D.

BRENDAN: You've had D. You've got 'and'. And-and-and! Somebody and somebody.

BRENDAN adds another line to the hangman drawing.

For fuck's sake! Oeo and Uet. It's one of them Shakespeare films.

JAY: I give up.

BRENDAN: (*Phonetically.*) O-ee-o and Oo-ee-et!

JAY looks at the board.

JAY: Boneo and coo…coolio?…stooly?…mooly? Mullet? Boneo and Mullet?

BRENDAN: You thick or what? I chose the poshest film I know cos I thought you was a clever sort.

BRENDAN adds the R. When he turns back to her, JAY is giggling.

You winding me up?

JAY: Only a little bit.

BRENDAN smiles.

BRENDAN: Fuck me, I thought you was a retard for a second then. So you do know it then?

JAY: We did Romeo and Juliet at school.

BRENDAN: You was in a play?

JAY: I was one of the Capulets. Had to run on with a sword and shout 'Death to all Montagues' and have a fight with a scabby bitch called Melanie Fulshaw. I hit her by accident and they had to amputate her thumb. Bad things happen to me Brendan. I don't know why, but they do.

BRENDAN: We watched the video with Maggie and she cried when Leonardo copped it. She's a romantic like me.

JAY: Yeah, I can tell.

BRENDAN: You got a boyfriend?

JAY: None of your business.

BRENDAN: I'm just being interested. Maggie says that's what people are supposed to be – interested in each other. Social interaction. That's how you get to know people, how you get girls to give you a go.

JAY: That how you're going to get her?

BRENDAN: Who?

JAY: Maggie. You've got a crush, it's obvious.

BRENDAN: Is it?

JAY: Yeah.

BRENDAN: So?

JAY: Not a chance.

BRENDAN: You never know what might happen. In a few years time, I might meet her at some party.

JAY: What kind of party?

BRENDAN: Dunno. A grown-up party.

JAY: Alright, let's suppose you manage to gatecrash this party and you spot Maggie on the far side of the room –

BRENDAN: Givin' out them sexy vibes.

JAY: She sees you.

BRENDAN: I'm checking her out.

JAY: Starts walking your way.

BRENDAN: All graceful, like a film star.

JAY: She's ten feet away, six –

BRENDAN: I'm cool as you like.

JAY: Mistake. Looks like she's going to walk straight past you – how d'you stop her?

BRENDAN: Dunno…spill my drink on her?

JAY sighs.

Ask her the time?… Bump into her?

JAY: Okay, so you bring her down with a rugby tackle, and?

BRENDAN looks at JAY thoughtfully a moment.

BRENDAN: Alright, I tell her I've been watching her for some time –

JAY: Too creepy.

BRENDAN: I smile sexily.

JAY: Show me.

BRENDAN smiles and raises an eyebrow.

BRENDAN: I say I'm bored with parties, would she like to have some fun?

JAY: Too frisky.

BRENDAN: There's a little bar I know. Very discreet.

JAY: *Now* she's interested.

BRENDAN: The pianist's a friend of mine.

JAY: Nice touch.

BRENDAN: They keep a bottle of champagne on ice for me. My Ferrari's out the front.

JAY: That'll do it.

BRENDAN: Touchdown! She's getting her coat. He shoots, he scores!

Beat.

JAY: So what now?

BRENDAN: Obvious isn'it? I take her back to my place and shag the shit out of her.

JAY: Nice.

BRENDAN: The perfect end to the perfect night.

JAY: S'pose we all got to have a dream.

BRENDAN: Could happen.

JAY: You don't really think she'd ever go with you.

BRENDAN: Why not?

JAY: 'Cos she's all loved up with that bloke.

BRENDAN: What bloke?

JAY: The bloke in charge.

BRENDAN: Tom?

JAY: Yeah, Tom.

BRENDAN: Don't be stupid.

JAY: They were all over each other this morning out back –

BRENDAN: (*Disbelieving.*) Tom?

JAY: Got his head on her shoulder, hands round her belly, rubbin' up –

BRENDAN: Nah-nah-nah, don't believe you. He's an old man –

JAY: So?

BRENDAN: Rubbin' against her?

JAY: Yeah, intimate.

BRENDAN: He's married.

JAY: Since when did that stop anyone?

Beat. BRENDAN's beginning to realise this isn't a wind-up.

BRENDAN: Straight up and promise?

JAY nods. BRENDAN scrutinises her face for hints of a lie before kicking out, incensed.

Fuck!

A beat as BRENDAN consider his options. He pulls out his mobile phone, a devilish grin growing on his face.

JAY: (*Concerned.*) What you doing?

BRENDAN flicks through his phone menus.

BRENDAN: D'you think it's right that a married man fucks round on his wife?

JAY: I dunno.

BRENDAN: You don't know what's right and what's wrong? Who brought you up? 'Tomhome'.

BRENDAN presses a button and puts the phone to his ear.

(*To JAY.*) For emergencies he said. If this isn't an emergency, I don't know what is.

JAY: I was telling you in confidence.

BRENDAN: You never said that.

JAY: Give me the phone Brendan.

BRENDAN jumps up onto the desk out of JAY's reach. And then someone answers –

BRENDAN: (*Best telephone voice.*) Hello? Is that the Marshall residence? …Am I speaking to Mrs Marshall?…

JAY realises what he plans to do…

JAY: Put it down!

But BRENDAN's not backing out and the grin returns.

BRENDAN: I've received some information about your husband Thomas…could you confirm whether the rumours of him having it away with a teacher at St. Peter's called Maggie Bates are true?…

Silence.

Mrs Marshall?… Mrs Marshall?…

BRENDAN's grin falls away. He seems genuinely upset.

(*With softened voice.*) Don't cry now. It was just a joke…don't cry…I'm sorry, I was just having a joke with you…I'm sorry…

BRENDAN clicks his phone off. A long silence.

We can't ever tell anyone about this. Not never.

Lights snap down on the classroom and up on…

7

TOM's office. MAGGIE and TOM are face to face. A suitcase sits on TOM's desk, a barrier between them.

MAGGIE: You'd better have a good explanation.

TOM: For what?

MAGGIE: For blowing me out last night, that's what.

TOM: I *tried* to ring you three times. Where did you go?

MAGGIE: When you didn't come, I went round to my sister's for some wine and a whinge.

But TOM is obviously shaken.

Tom, what's happened?

TOM: Someone rang Hazel yesterday.

Beat.

Told her about me and you. I got home at six and she was roosting on the sofa with a triple gin and that witch Judy from next door.

MAGGIE: Who would do that, who would tell?

TOM: I have no idea. Someone must have seen us.

MAGGIE: They couldn't have.

TOM: Well it wasn't a lucky guess.

Beat.

MAGGIE: What did you say to her?

TOM: You want to know everything?

MAGGIE: Did you admit it, deny it, what?

TOM: I told her I was in love with you.

MAGGIE: Oh Tom –

TOM: What?

MAGGIE: The poor woman didn't need to hear that.

TOM: I didn't want to lie anymore.

MAGGIE: But to talk about love –

TOM: You think it would have helped if I'd said you meant nothing? That I'd thrown away our marriage for nothing?

Beat.

Anyway, she wouldn't let me stay so I had to sleep here. Popped out for some milk at six and found this on the front steps. (*TOM indicates the suitcase.*) She must have driven it over.

MAGGIE: Poor Hazel, she must have been up all night.

TOM: That's a bit rich –

MAGGIE: Sorry?

TOM: All this poor Hazel nonsense. You knew the situation.

MAGGIE: Yes, you're right, I did.

A gloomy silence as they both think.

TOM: We've got to look on the bright side: this may all be for the best.

MAGGIE: How can this possibly be for the best?

TOM: She had to be told at some point. It's not the way I would have chosen, but it's done now. It's not as if we never talked about our future together –

MAGGIE: We talked, yes –

TOM: Then maybe this happened for a reason.

MAGGIE: Christ Tom, has it come to this?

TOM: What?

MAGGIE: Falling back on some half-arsed fatalism –

TOM: I'm just saying it might be for the best in the long run.

MAGGIE: Don't be so bloody witless. How can it be for the best that some malicious bastard cold-calls your wife to tell her you're shagging someone she knows and trusts? What a bloody mess!

Beat.

MAGGIE: (*Calmer.*) So what are you going to do now?

TOM: I need to find somewhere to stay.

MAGGIE: (*Interpreting his look.*) It's not a good idea.

TOM: Why not?

MAGGIE: Because I'm not prepared to do that.

TOM: So you can have an affair, but when it all goes belly-up, you're not 'prepared' to help me out.

MAGGIE: (*Cold.*) No, I'm not.

TOM: Can I ask why?

MAGGIE: Because it's not what I had planned.

TOM: Because it's not what you had planned. And you think I planned this?

MAGGIE: According to you, some divine being planned this! Well, I'm afraid I'm not buying that. It doesn't have to be this way.

TOM: So I have to sleep in my office like a bloody tramp?

MAGGIE: There are hotels Tom.

TOM: I don't want to be in a hotel, I want to be with you.

MAGGIE: I'm thirty three years old and I've always lived on my own – *chosen* to live on my own. I'm not going to be rushed into giving that up. I'm sorry, I'm just not.

TOM: But we'd talked about it.

MAGGIE: I've talked about lots of things, trekking through the Andes and buying run-down houses in France – but I've never actually done them.

TOM: So it was all just a game.

MAGGIE: (*Warming.*) No Tom, it wasn't. But I never really thought it would happen, not really, and it's taken this to make me see that. I'm sorry.

A knock at the door.

TOM: Come in.

JAY enters. Sensing the frosty atmosphere, and guessing at her part in creating it, she seems dumbstruck.

What is it Jay?

JAY: There's a man at the front gate. Mary sent me to get you.

Beat.

TOM: (*Curt.*) What does he want?

JAY: To see you.

TOM: I know that for Christ's sake!

MAGGIE: (*Warmly.*) Does he need to see Tom right now?

JAY: He's got some plants.

MAGGIE: Tom'll be straight down.

JAY turns to leave.

Thanks Jay.

JAY exits.

TOM: Well that's just brilliant –

MAGGIE: Don't take it out on the students Tom, please.

TOM: You really do have a low opinion of me, don't you.

MAGGIE: Why don't you go home and sort things out?

TOM: Because I've got an appeal meeting tonight and two vultures from the LEA due in tomorrow. And now I've got a garden to plant.

MAGGIE: The garden can wait.

TOM: (*Aping her words.*) 'But it'll make such a positive impact on our friends from the council'. And I've just spent two hundred quid getting it delivered.

TOM gets up to leave.

MAGGIE: I could go to Orlando's appeal for you if it helps.

TOM: You're just a teacher here Maggie. Remember that.

TOM exits, slamming the door. MAGGIE stares blankly ahead. Shell-shocked. Lights down.

8

The garden. Bright sun. BRENDAN lies on the newly-laid grass. JAY busies herself weeding. TOM is digging a hole downstage whilst PATSY examines a collection of plants and shrubs that sit ready to be planted.

TOM: Are you just going to lie there?

BRENDAN: Do I look like Alan fuckin' Titchmarsh?

PATSY holds up a small pot of jasmine.

PATSY: What's this mean? Andro someink.

TOM: Sorry?

PATSY: Andro – someink weird.

TOM: Androsace pubescens. It's the plant's name –

BRENDAN: Ha ha.

PATSY: Shut up Brendan.

BRENDAN: 'Kay 'kay.

TOM: Every plant has two names, the common name – this one's called Rock Jasmine, yes? – and the botanical name, a posh name –

PATSY: S'like me. Patsy or Patricia –

TOM: Sort of, yes.

BRENDAN: Like Superman.

TOM: Yeah Brendan, like Superman.

PATSY: Androsace.

TOM: That's the name of the family, the genus.

PATSY: (*Struggling.*) Pubes –

BRENDAN: Ha ha.

PATSY: Fuck off Brendan.

TOM: Pubescens. That tells you the species. It means hairy.

PATSY: Why don't they jus' write it in English?

BRENDAN: Patsyus Pubescens innit –

TOM: Not everybody speaks English. This way nobody gets confused.

BRENDAN: My name is Maximus Decimus Meridius and this is my wife Patsyus Pussyus Pubescens. And I *will* have her snatch, in this life or the next –

TOM: That's enough.

LANNY enters carrying a potted bay tree. He places it on the ground.

What's that?

LANNY: A tree.

PATSY: What's its name?

LANNY: It don't have a name, it's a tree.

PATSY: All plants got names.

PATSY examines the label.

TOM: This for the garden Lanny?

LANNY: (*Embarrassed.*) Yeah.

PATSY: Laurus nobless.

BRENDAN: Ha ha.

TOM: Laurus nobilis. It's a bay tree. Thank you Lanny.

LANNY: S'alright.

PATSY: £15.99!

LANNY: Someone gave it me.

BRENDAN: Ha ha! You tiefin' bastard.

> *TOM rips the label off the tree and puts it in his pocket.*

TOM: It's a lovely thought Lanny. Now let's get it in the ground. You're making a good job of that weeding Jay –

PATSY: Why we doing this anyway, there should be a gardener or someink –

TOM: Thought you might enjoy the challenge.

BRENDAN: It's for those inspectors innit. Make the place look sorted.

TOM: Don't you want somewhere nice to sit in the summer?

BRENDAN: Be like the Garden of Eden. What d'you think Jay?

PATSY: What you on about?

BRENDAN: The garden from the Bible.

PATSY: Noah and all that shit.

BRENDAN: (*Priest-like.*) And the Lord God took the man – Adam right? – and put him into the garden of Eden to keep it nice blah-di-blah. And he says 'Of every tree of the garden thou mayest freely eat: But of the tree of the knowledge of good and evil, thou shalt not eat of it: for in the day that thou eatest thereof thou shalt surely die.'

TOM: The original sin.

BRENDAN: See? If it wasn't for Eve we'd be running round a perfect garden, wagglin' our bits and –

PATSY: You get your dick out and I'll kill you.

MAGGIE comes in and sits on the grass.

TOM: You've decided to come and join the workers then?

MAGGIE: Thought I'd see how it's coming on.

TOM: We were just talking about the possible similarities between our new school garden and the Garden of Eden.

MAGGIE: We'll have to give all the plants and animals new names.

TOM: You've lost me.

BRENDAN: That's what happened in Eden. God called up all the birds and animals and shit, and Adam gave them all names.

TOM: I'd forgotten that. Named them to show that he owned them.

LANNY: What you on about now?

BRENDAN: If we're making our very own Eden, we should be able to name everything for the first time.

JAY: Like we were explorers.

MAGGIE: Yeah, just pretend you're explorers and imagine you're all like Adam finding a brand new land.

TOM: Spots a link to the English curriculum and she's off.

MAGGIE: (*Ignores him.*) You've been walking round all day long in the heat, looking at the plants, examining the soil, making notes –

BRENDAN: On what?

MAGGIE: Alright, alright. Suddenly you see this little creature poke its nose out of a bush. It's got a beak like a bird, but has claws like a cat. Its feet are webbed, but its body's covered in fur like a dog or a badger –

BRENDAN: Or a beaver?

MAGGIE: (*Warily.*) Okay, like a beaver.

BRENDAN: I love beavers! Beavers are fuckin' A –

TOM: Tread carefully, I smell blood.

MAGGIE: The creature's old or ill or just plain tired and you bend down to pick her up, to help her. But she thinks you're attacking and bites you on the hand. Only it's not just a bite, because you feel a sharp hot pain racing up your arm –

PATSY: It's poison innit.

MAGGIE: Yep.

BRENDAN: A poisonous beaver, what are the chances of that, eh Tom?

MAGGIE: You've been bitten by something and you don't even know what it is. Then, because you're a responsible type, you start thinking about what might happen if Eve found one of these cute little monsters –

PATSY: It'd fuck her up.

TOM: Patsy –

MAGGIE: Bigtime. So you've got to let the world know about this beaverduckcatsnakething. It needs a name. What would you call it?

BRENDAN: Trevor.

MAGGIE: Seriously.

BRENDAN: I would seriously call it a Trevor.

MAGGIE: Any more suggestions?

LANNY: A poisonous some'ink.

MAGGIE: Yep.

BRENDAN: What's wrong with Trevor?

MAGGIE: There's nothing wrong with Trevor.

PATSY: A poisonous beaverbeak.

LANNY: A poisonous *clawed* beaverbeak.

TOM: Maggie said you'd never seen a beaver, never seen the beak of a duck or a swan or anything. What would you call it then? Brendan? (*BRENDAN is sulking.*) Jay? (*JAY shrugs.*) Think about what it does.

PATSY: It fucks you up.

LANNY: Looks like a duck.

PATSY: It fucks you up.

LANNY: Looks like a duck.

PATSY: Duckfuck. Fuckyduck.

LANNY: Beaverfuckyduck.

PATSY: Hairyduckfucker.

PATSY collapses in laughter.

JAY: You're not doing it right.

PATSY: What?

JAY: He said you didn't know what a duck was.

PATSY: So?

JAY: You can't call it a hairyduckthingie if you don't know what a duck is first.

PATSY: What d'you call it then shitbox?

JAY: You might as well call it a Trevor.

PATSY: Why the fuck would you call it a Trevor?

MAGGIE: Look, this was just meant to be a bit of fun –

TOM: I'm saying nothing, I'm just the gardener.

BRENDAN: A Trevorneal. (*Tre-vorr-nee-al.*)

MAGGIE: Sounds good, but what does it mean?

BRENDAN: The Trevorneal is the male of the species. Hunts down the female from the scent of her poisonous beaver and gets her nips out in the back of his Mazda.

PATSY kicks out.

LANNY: Ha ha.

PATSY: It ain't funny Lanny.

LANNY: I know it ain't.

Pause.

TOM: Now *this* is interesting. We're in a very familiar land now aren't we? So how d'you *feel* now Patsy?

PATSY: What?

TOM: We've all got to be in tune with our feelings, isn't that right Maggie?

MAGGIE: (*Warily.*) If you say so.

TOM: I do. So how d'you feel Patsy?

PATSY: Fucked off.

TOM: There we go. Fucked off. Is that all?

77

BRENDAN: Aroused.

PATSY: I'll arouse you in a minute you damp little prick.

TOM: You're embarrassed, yes?

PATSY: Nah, I ain't.

TOM: But you're angry.

PATSY: I'm fucked off.

TOM: So you're angry with Brendan.

PATSY: And bitch there for startin' this. And Lanny cos he's laughin'.

LANNY: I weren't laughin' at you.

TOM: Are you angry with me? With Maggie?

PATSY: I'm jus' fucked off.

TOM: So you're just fucked off with the world in general.

PATSY: Yeah. I hate the fuckin' lot of you!

MAGGIE: (*Warning.*) Tom...

TOM: We're exploring Patsy's anger. Miss Bates has read books on this, haven't you? It's all good stuff.

PATSY: I don't want to explore my anger.

PATSY gives a reluctant smile.

TOM: We all know what Patsy's feeling, don't we?

Beat.

It's like a volcano erupting deep inside you and no matter how much you try to stop it, there's nowhere else for that anger to go – it's got to come out. It's like an explosion. Or a tidal wave. Something massive and unstoppable and completely outside your control. What can you call a feeling like that?

LANNY: It's jus' feelin' angry innit.

TOM: Is it? One minute you're laughing and joking, the next – BOOM!

BRENDAN: Yeah, boom – s'like someone pulls a trigger.

LANNY: Yeah, s'like you're the gun.

TOM: And you can't stop it. Like someone *else* has pulled a trigger.

BRENDAN: Like a tidal wave.

LANNY: Like a volcano.

TOM: Let's try Miss Bates' approach. Imagine you didn't have a word for a feeling like that. You want to tell someone else, to explain, to somehow express what you're feeling at the very moment when it all explodes.

LANNY: It's just angry.

TOM: But when most people feel angry, they don't attack people or throw things –

TOM roars 'Fuck!' and hurls the pot of jasmine off-stage. The kids look startled.

MAGGIE: There's no need for that.

TOM: Sorry?

MAGGIE: No need.

TOM: I'm just dramatising their anger, engaging them in the task, focusing them on their learning objective –

MAGGIE: I think it's time I took them inside.

TOM: No, leave them. They like it out here. So 'kids' what do we call it when we get angry like that?

BRENDAN: Red mist.

TOM: Okay, so why do people call it red mist?

BRENDAN: Red mist…pissed….pissed off.

JAY: Red means danger, anger, violence. It's like blood and wars and stuff like that –

JAY loses confidence.

TOM: Go on.

JAY: So when people say they've got red mist, it's like their vision, everything in their world, it turns red and they can't see anything else for a while – it's all blood and killing and hurting and death.

Beat.

TOM: What d'you all think of that?

PATSY: S'bollocks. I ain't got no red mist.

BRENDAN: I got somethin' red and *massive*.

PATSY: You *wish*.

TOM: D'you see? People make up new ways of saying things because the old ways, they just don't quite explain the way they feel. It's like when you say something's *bad*, that means it's really, really *good*. So I could say Miss Bates is a really bad person and I might mean she was really good and I really liked her –

BRENDAN: Or you say she's really *fat*.

TOM: So, she's fat and bad, so she's good.

MAGGIE: I don't think we should be talking about me here.

LANNY: If you thought she was *really* good, she'd be badnuff.

PATSY: Like I seen this boy walking down the street and his arse, it was badnuff!

TOM: Oh, I think Miss Bates is totally badnuff.

BRENDAN: Steady Tom, steady.

TOM: And what about when you feel angry? Jay? You ever felt angry? I'll bet you have.

But JAY is silent.

Lanny? You're our resident angry young man. Describe your feelings as the world turns red.

LANNY: I told you, that's just angry.

TOM: Yeah, alright you can say you feel angry, but if it doesn't quite capture that feeling, the speed of your anger, the violence, maybe even the *reasons* –

PATSY: You tryin' to teach us somethink here?

TOM holds up his hands – 'as if I'd try'.

LANNY: Volcanger.

PATSY: You losin' it Lanny or what?

LANNY: S'like anger, but it's unstoppable, like a volcano.

TOM: You hear that? Volcanger. Lanny's taken two words and pushed them together to make a new one. Those words are like two cars colliding at a hundred miles an hour and, if they hit dead on, you'll never pull them apart. All the metal's twisted together and the heat's welded the chassis and the engines and the bodies are linked together forever –

BRENDAN: So both cars are fucked.

PATSY: What you on about?

TOM: Maggie, you're the expert d'you want to explain?

MAGGIE: (*Shading her anger.*) I can't explain, but I think what Lanny said was really clever. Come on now, inside.

The kids get up to leave.

TOM: My wife's really angry with me at the moment, I mean *really* angry.

LANNY: Mrs Tom, she's like a volcano!

PATSY: She's a tidal wave.

LANNY: You not been doing the washing up Mr?

TOM: Something like that.

PATSY: You ought to make her explore her anger innit.

TOM: Maybe I will Patsy, maybe I will.

As they exit, TOM takes MAGGIE aside as JAY looks on.

You like my new approach?

MAGGIE: You're being pathetic.

TOM: I love you.

MAGGIE: No you don't.

MAGGIE walks away, takes JAY's shoulder and guides her upstage.

Come on Jay, Tom's got lots of work to do.

They leave. TOM lashes out at a few plants and slumps to the floor.

9

The classroom. PATSY stands nervously.

PATSY: I done my writing like as if it was happening to someone else. Like a story.

MAGGIE: You decided to write it in the third person.

PATSY: Nah, it's just about me.

MAGGIE: (*Smiling.*) Good.

PATSY: Do I have to stand up?

MAGGIE: Not if you don't want to.

PATSY: I want to.

PATSY shuffles nervously, her essay in hand.

Nah, I feel too big.

She sits. Shuffles her essay. LANNY starts a slow hand-clap.

Alright Lanny, keep your fuckin' hair on!

PATSY clears her throat.

(*Reading.*) Patsy was born in Kent on 12 September at the end of the twentieth century. She come out of her mum so quick the doctor said it was like catching a seal fired out of a cannon –

BRENDAN smirks. PATSY shoots him daggers but continues. MAGGIE moves to sit by BRENDAN to quash further outbursts.

Patsy was a slim baby with nice skin. Her mother called Jeanette was upset because she didn't have any hair. But luckily it growed. Patsy always liked drinking from an early age and her first word was 'beena', which meant Ribena. But she wasn't thick, she just didn't hear the name of the drink right –

BRENDAN: (*Baby-voice.*) Little Patsy-watsy want her beena-weena?

PATSY: Fuck off!

MAGGIE: Okay Patsy, now Brendan you've got to be quiet.

BRENDAN: Sorry chief. It's zipped.

BRENDAN draws the imaginary mouth-zip closed.

MAGGIE: Patsy?

PATSY: (*Deflated.*) That's it. That's all I got.

MAGGIE: You've got a couple of pages there.

PATSY: They're notes.

Beat. But PATSY won't change her mind.

MAGGIE: Okay. Your turn Brendan.

BRENDAN: Ain't done it.

MAGGIE: Nothing?

BRENDAN: Not a word.

MAGGIE: Fine. It's your exam. No work. No marks.

BRENDAN seems disappointed that MAGGIE lets him off without a fight.

Next up we've got Lanny.

LANNY folds the piece of paper on his desk and places it in his jacket.

LANNY: Nah.

MAGGIE: You don't have to be shy.

LANNY: I ain't shy.

BRENDAN: Memoirs of a Batty Boy –

MAGGIE: Shut up Brendan. Come on Lanny, I know you've written a few paragraphs –

PATSY: He has, I saw it.

MAGGIE: I'm marking you for speaking and listening remember, so if you don't speak –

LANNY shakes his head, embarrassed.

No-one's going to laugh at you, I promise.

PATSY: Go on Lanny.

MAGGIE: It's important.

LANNY: (*Indicating BRENDAN.*) Not in front of him.

MAGGIE: I can't just make Brendan vanish.

LANNY: He could stand outside.

BRENDAN: I ain't goin' nowhere.

MAGGIE: I want Brendan to hear what you've written.

LANNY: He don't give out the marks.

MAGGIE: I want him to hear it because it might help him understand you. I want you to listen to his autobiography for the same reason – when he gets round to writing it.

LANNY: He'll just laugh.

MAGGIE: He won't laugh at you because he'll respect the fact that you're doing a brave thing, isn't that right Brendan?

BRENDAN: Yeah.

PATSY: And that you'll fuck him up if he takes the piss.

MAGGIE: Patsy –

PATSY: Sorry.

BRENDAN: Look, I won't say nothing. Promise.

Pause.

LANNY: Why don't you read it out?

MAGGIE: Because I'm assessing you.

LANNY: (*To BRENDAN.*) You better not laugh.

BRENDAN: Not one giggle.

LANNY deliberately unfolds the sheet of A4 paper. Looks up at BRENDAN again.

LANNY: (*Reading.*) When I was five our house caught on fire and the fireman rescued me from the bedroom.

LANNY looks cautiously over to BRENDAN who remains expressionless.

My brother jumped out the window and broke his leg so that the bone came out of the skin on his leg. That's the first thing I can remember. We moved to Hackney when I was seven or eight and I started at the school there. My best friend was Danny Bates, but we called him Magic because he thought he could do magic. One time he tried to turn water into whisky, only it was whisky all along that he'd nicked off of his Dad. I drank it and puked up on his Mum's best settee. We knew he wasn't magic when he couldn't magic away the puke. Danny went to live in Wales with his Auntie and I never saw him again. My Mum is called Josie. My brother's called Darius. My Dad's called Wesley. He lives somewhere in Hendon with some woman and their two daughters, Kylie and Shanice. I was born in Archway. I was called Orlando because of the woman who was in the hospital bed next to my mum. She told my mum about this book where there's a boy that turns into a girl, or a girl that turns into a boy. Before she had me, my Mum always thought that I was going to be a girl and that's why she called me –

BRENDAN chokes back a laugh, but too late. LANNY throws down the piece of paper.

BRENDAN: I'm not laughin' –

But he's smiling. LANNY gets up angrily and walks toward the door.

MAGGIE: (*Screaming at BRENDAN.*) You hateful little bastard!

BRENDAN: Fuckin' hell, who stuck a rocket up *your* arse?

LANNY runs full pelt at BRENDAN, knocking him to the floor. LANNY straddles his body and begins pounding BRENDAN's face with his fists. As BRENDAN screams, MAGGIE tries to haul LANNY off him but he's too strong. He just carries on pummelling BRENDAN, blow after blow, the sickening sound of bone pounding flesh. Finally, MAGGIE manages to pull him off and LANNY collapses heavily on the floor. BRENDAN lies staring at the ceiling, his chest heaving up and down exaggeratedly. MAGGIE crouches by BRENDAN's side and examines his face.

MAGGIE: Can you move your neck?

BRENDAN: Yes, of course I can move my neck, he was twatting me in the fuckin' face.

BRENDAN touches his nose tentatively. There's blood on his hands.

I think he broke my nose. You hear that you filthy black bastard? You broke my fuckin' nose!

MAGGIE: That's enough now Brendan, just lie still.

JAY: Should I go and get someone?

MAGGIE: No, let me just think this through for a second.

JAY: He's been hit in the head.

MAGGIE: I *know* he's been hit in the head Jay. Let me think!

Silence.

LANNY: (*Quietly, a cry.*) Oh God...

BRENDAN: Who's crying? Don't tell me it's him, don't tell me he's fuckin' crying! What you cryin' for you big black cunt? Come and finish me off you fuckin' black poof!

PATSY: Don't call him that.

BRENDAN: I'll call him whatever I want.

JAY goes to the door.

JAY: I'm going to get Tom –

MAGGIE: You can't, he isn't there… I think he's in a meeting. Brendan, can you sit up?

BRENDAN: Yeah.

BRENDAN sits up groggily.

PATSY: We could call an ambulance.

MAGGIE: He doesn't need an ambulance.

JAY: How d'you know?

MAGGIE pulls out a pack of tissues.

MAGGIE: I just know. Now will you Jay, and you Patsy, just get out of here for a moment.

PATSY: I ain't goin' nowhere.

MAGGIE: Get out!

PATSY: Alright, alright, keep your fuckin' hair on.

MAGGIE: And not a word about this, not to anyone.

JAY and PATSY leave reluctantly. MAGGIE begins to wipe the blood from BRENDAN's face.

BRENDAN: I know what you want.

MAGGIE: What's that?

BRENDAN: You want me to keep schtum.

MAGGIE: What makes you think that?

BRENDAN: 'Cos you like him best.

MAGGIE: Don't be so silly.

BRENDAN: Okay, tell me it's not true then. Tell me you like us just the same.

MAGGIE: I'm your teacher, I don't have favourites.

BRENDAN: Yeah, you do.

Beat.

I want to speak to Tom.

MAGGIE: Why?

BRENDAN: (*Disbelieving.*) Why?

MAGGIE: I can sort this out.

BRENDAN: No, you can't.

LANNY has got to his feet.

Where you going?

LANNY: I'll go and tell him.

MAGGIE: (*Firm.*) Sit down Orlando.

LANNY sits.

BRENDAN: Why you so bothered about Tom knowing?

MAGGIE: It's got nothing to do with Tom.

BRENDAN: It's *his* school, I'm his student and I've just been assaulted!

MAGGIE: Calm down, okay?

BRENDAN: You lookin' forward to that appeal meeting tonight Lanny? Wonder what they'll make of all this?

MAGGIE fixes him hard.

LANNY: (*Half-whisper.*) I don't care what they think no more.

BRENDAN: Lanny, you lie.

MAGGIE: Okay Brendan, can we cut the shit please? What d'you want?

BRENDAN: For what?

MAGGIE: To keep quiet about this.

BRENDAN: See, there you go.

MAGGIE: What?

BRENDAN: He beats me up, but you're still prepared to do stuff to help him.

MAGGIE: It's taken a lot of work to persuade Lanny's school to give him this chance, and I don't want some silly argument to ruin it.

BRENDAN: Would you do the same for me? Would you? If I needed your time, would you give me it?

MAGGIE: But you don't.

BRENDAN: Yes, I do.

MAGGIE: Then yes, I'll give you my time.

BRENDAN: At your flat? Would you give me your private time at *your* private place?

MAGGIE: Why would you want to – ?

BRENDAN: Because I want you to like me the same as him!

Pause.

MAGGIE: And we just forget all about this?

BRENDAN: If you like.

Beat.

MAGGIE: Then yes Brendan, I will.

Lights snap off.

10

The garden. Brilliant sun. The garden is finished. TOM and PATSY lie on the grass. JAY sits on the swing.

TOM: Shall I tell you a love story?

PATSY: Long as it's not pervy.

TOM: It's not pervy at all. In fact, it's the most beautiful story I ever heard. It's the story that made me want to be a teacher.

PATSY: If it gets pervy I'm telling my mum.

TOM: Fine, you do that. (*Beat.*) Long time ago, sometime in the 1930s, the Russian government carried out an experiment. They took two babies from an orphanage, a boy and a girl, and kept them locked in a room –

PATSY: That happened to some kids on our estate.

TOM: Not like this it didn't.

PATSY: Yeah, they was locked in a room –

TOM: This room was in a warehouse, a secret warehouse in the middle of nowhere. Up to the age of three, the children were fed and changed by nurses, and these nurses had been told to carry out their duties quickly and silently – no smiles, no frowns, no touching unless it was really necessary – and after ten days work, the nurses left so the children couldn't bond with them. Soon as these kids hit three years old, the scientists, or psychologists or whatever, stopped sending the nurses into the room completely. The only thing they were taught was how to find the food that was left for them, and they were left alone. Completely alone.

PATSY: That's child abuse that is.

TOM: Yes, it was.

PATSY: Why didn't no-one stop it?

TOM: Because the scientists wanted to study how the children would turn out if they grew up in a world without love. They wanted to study all the children's experiences, and end up with a formula that they could take to their leaders and say this is how love works, this is how to make love grow inside people.

PATSY: Like plants innit.

TOM: Yeah, and all this time they were observing, developing theories and testing them over and over again. They left gifts that might appeal to one of the children so they could watch to see if they shared stuff or kept it to themselves, the in-built tendency toward love or hate…constantly straining, straining to peel back the layers and find the core, the essence, of love. And then one day, they found it.

Beat.

JAY: What?

PATSY turns – she'd forgotten JAY was there and certainly didn't think she was paying attention.

TOM: The experiment had been running for five years. One morning the scientists came to work as usual. They took up their observation posts and tried to find the children, but they'd gone. Disappeared. Two five year old children had just vanished into thin air. So they started searching. I mean, how could two tiny children get far? But no luck. They looked harder, called in the army, broke down doors and ransacked all the homes, farms, churches within a hundred miles. A whole week passed before they finally found the children, huddled in a grain store with a woman called Anna.

PATSY: Who's this Anna?

TOM: Anna was a cook. She'd been preparing the children's meals from the beginning. Anna knew all about the experiment, and she also knew what would happen to anyone who broke the rules. And so it happened: Anna was executed, just as she knew she would be.

PATSY: What happened to the kiddies?

TOM: They'd been exposed to the outside world, so the scientists had no more use for them and returned them to an orphanage. The government had set out to find how love worked. And Anna had shown them.

Pause. JAY has been crying and she wipes her eyes quickly.

PATSY: I don't get it.

TOM: She sacrificed herself for love.

PATSY: Right, so some old cook stole the abused kiddies and got fucked over for it – why you telling us this bullshit story?

TOM: Because I was thinking about it, and it made me sad.

PATSY: The kiddies got rescued, didn't they?

TOM: No, I'm not sad about the story so much. I'm sad because ever since I first heard it, I'd thought that if I was in Anna's position, I'd do exactly what she did. But now I'm not so sure.

Lights fade down.

11

MAGGIE's flat. MAGGIE and BRENDAN sit together at the table. MAGGIE has a pen and a notebook. BRENDAN's face is bruised and swollen.

BRENDAN: You got some nice stuff here.

MAGGIE: Thank you Brendan.

BRENDAN: Stylish.

MAGGIE: I try.

BRENDAN: Like your curtains.

MAGGIE: Let's get on. I want you back home by ten.

BRENDAN: I don't see how I can write about my life if nothing's ever happened to me.

MAGGIE: Take it step by step. Start off with where you were born.

BRENDAN: The Royal.

MAGGIE makes a note. She continues to do so throughout the sequence.

MAGGIE: See, we're up and running.

BRENDAN: I was a caesarian baby.

MAGGIE: That's good.

BRENDAN: Apparently my Dad said I didn't want to come out, and he wished the doctors had listened to me.

MAGGIE: I can see where you get your sense of humour from.

BRENDAN: Yeah, right.

MAGGIE: So now, earliest memories – what was the first thing you remember?

BRENDAN: Dunno.

MAGGIE: Think.

Pause.

BRENDAN: Falling out the back of a car?

MAGGIE: How old?

BRENDAN: Nine, ten.

MAGGIE: You must remember stuff before that.

BRENDAN: I was a shepherd in the school nativity. I had to say 'Lo, the boy king awakes.' And then we all kneeled down, only it wasn't as good as it should have been 'cos Darren Pye had pissed on my toy lamb so I was carrying a white cricket jumper instead.

MAGGIE: You can turn it into a funny story with the lamb and everything. When was that?

BRENDAN: Dunno, when I was about seven?

MAGGIE: Nothing before that?

BRENDAN: Nah.

MAGGIE: Okay. So now what about your family? Dad?

BRENDAN: Kevin Casey.

MAGGIE: Mum?

BRENDAN: Denise.

MAGGIE: But you don't live with them, is that right?

BRENDAN: I've lived with my Auntie since I was six.

MAGGIE: That's Auntie Babs, yes? And you moved in with her after your parents separated?

BRENDAN: They haven't separated, least no-one told me if they have.

MAGGIE: So –

BRENDAN: I don't know what went on, alright?

MAGGIE: Maybe we should leave this section.

BRENDAN: You want me to write about my life. Can't hardly write about it without talking about my parents can I?

MAGGIE: I don't want you getting upset.

BRENDAN: Nah, don't want things getting messy.

MAGGIE: If it's too distressing, we can just stop.

BRENDAN: I'm not distressed, it's dead simple. My mum and dad went on a trip to America to see some relative who lived out in New York. Left me with my Auntie. Three weeks they said. Only three weeks came and went and they never showed. My Auntie rings the relative. Strange he says, they left here ten days ago. Said they were going to some other town, some place where there was lots of building going on, somewhere my Dad could find work.

MAGGIE: And they never came back?

BRENDAN: Nah.

MAGGIE: You never heard from them?

BRENDAN: Auntie Babs said my Dad got himself in some trouble with some blokes from Deptford. Scared to come back she reckons.

Beat.

BRENDAN: Guaranteed one hundred per cent non-fiction.

MAGGIE: I'm sorry Brendan.

BRENDAN: What for? Ain't your fault.

MAGGIE: I'm sorry that happened to you.

The door bell rings. MAGGIE goes to the window and peeps out.

Oh shit.

BRENDAN: What?

MAGGIE: It's Tom. Just stay quiet.

The door bell rings again. And again. MAGGIE gets up and goes to the entry-phone.

Wait in the kitchen while I talk to him.

BRENDAN: Why?

MAGGIE presses the buzzer to let TOM in. BRENDAN hesitates.

MAGGIE: Just go Brendan, please.

BRENDAN exits and MAGGIE clears up the notepad and hides BRENDAN's jacket. A knock at the door. She opens it and TOM stumbles inside, clearly very drunk and holding a semi-wrapped kebab.

TOM: I was just passing –

MAGGIE: You can't stay Tom.

TOM: Just thought we could have a little talk.

MAGGIE: Okay, would you like to sit down?

TOM: I'd prefer to stand.

MAGGIE: I'd feel more comfortable if you sat.

TOM: Well, we can't always have what we want.

Beat.

MAGGIE: How on earth did you get in this state? You don't drink…

TOM: I don't eat kebabs either –

TOM looks at the kebab in a puzzled fashion.

Have you eaten?

MAGGIE: Yes, yes, I have. How did Orlando's meeting go?

TOM: I'm sure it went fine. I told you, it'll be a shoe-in.

MAGGIE: You didn't go?

TOM: I was going, but at the last minute I had a thought, and that thought was 'fuck it'. 'Thuck it' I fought –

TOM smirks at his slip of the tongue. But MAGGIE isn't amused.

MAGGIE: You said you would go. I trusted you.

TOM: You said we could live together. Evidently people don't always stand by what they say.

MAGGIE: So what now?

TOM: I don't know. What now?

MAGGIE: We'll have to ring Larkhill first thing, make sure it didn't harm Lanny's case –

TOM: Look, I couldn't give a flying fuck about Lanny-Danny-Stanny or any of the ungrateful tossers who've traipsed through my gates with their greasy hair and their –

MAGGIE: Tom, will you please keep your voice down –

TOM: Fifteen years I've been doing this, and I could count the number of thank-yous on one hand. Fifteen years of marking the crap our kids churn out and telling them it's gold because we mustn't let them become disaffected – I mean, that's a joke isn't it? Disaffected? I'm the fucking disaffected one!

MAGGIE: You're being ridiculous –

TOM: Yeah, I am, but d'you want to know what's really ridiculous? People like you telling me that, after fifteen years working with kids like these, my approach is wrong. Everyone thinks they have the answer, but they forget the question.

MAGGIE: Which is?

TOM: What is the most effective way to sterilise society's shit?

MAGGIE: Now you're being stupid.

TOM: Am I?

MAGGIE: Yes, and you know you are.

TOM: See, you won't even acknowledge a basic truth.

MAGGIE: That the kids we teach are what...shit? That's a disgusting thing to say.

TOM: Okay, I admit it, unlike you I'm not exactly steeped in the latest PC terminology –

MAGGIE: So now I'm some woolly liberal? It's just so lazy –

TOM: Listen Maggie. Some people are just born bad. It's as simple as that.

MAGGIE: I don't believe you think that.

TOM: Some of our kids have had terrible things happen to them, horrific, unimaginable things. But terrible things happen to lots of people and they don't stick two fingers up at society and go on the rampage.

MAGGIE: Just listen to yourself Tom. You've just spent five minutes ramming two fingers down my throat, so what's your excuse?

A long beat.

TOM: The woman I love doesn't want me.

MAGGIE: Stop saying that –

TOM: What? Love?

MAGGIE: You don't love me.

TOM closes in on her. MAGGIE backs away.

TOM: Love-love-love-love-love-love-love...yes I do, I do. I love you so much I feel like my chest's been ripped open and every dirty bastard I see on the street, in the pub, in every shop, they can all see...

MAGGIE: Tom, I'd like you to leave.

TOM: Not until you tell me that's it.

MAGGIE: We can talk when you're sober –

TOM: Is that it then Maggie? Tell me –

MAGGIE: Tom, please leave –

BRENDAN enters the room. He holds a large saucepan.

BRENDAN: She said you gotta go.

TOM can't believe it. He backs away from MAGGIE. Laughs wryly to himself.

TOM: I didn't know you were in the habit of taking your work home with you.

MAGGIE: He asked for some help with his work.

TOM: You never told me Brendan was a model student. I remember us laughing about him only yesterday. Funny to think you can be laughing at him one minute, inviting him over to your flat the next –

MAGGIE: It was just homework.

TOM: As in his home, not yours. Either that or I've been getting it wrong my whole career. You doing a bit of cooking Brendan? Cooking up something tasty?

BRENDAN: You just keep it coming –

TOM: Well that's big talk from a little man. How d'you get those bruises anyhow? Miss Bates getting a bit kinky was she?

BRENDAN screams and lunges at TOM, the frying pan raised to strike. MAGGIE grabs him. BRENDAN struggles, but she manages to restrain him.

Well, as your employer Miss Bates, I think I'm obliged to check out what the handbooks have to say about inappropriate contact. I've got a file on Child Protection this thick –

TOM spreads his fingers wide.

MAGGIE: And I'm sure you've got one on sexual harassment in the workplace.

Beat. TOM shakes his head, smiles.

TOM: You signed up with a union Miss Bates?

MAGGIE: Oh yeah.

TOM: Good. Game on then.

TOM turns to go.

I'll be ringing your Auntie as soon as I step outside Brendan. Check she knows where you are. Enjoy your evening.

TOM exits. MAGGIE lets BRENDAN go and collapses into a chair. BRENDAN just stands, unsure of what to do to help her.

Lights down.

12

The classroom. The following day. MAGGIE is emptying the contents of her desk into a crate as PATSY comes in.

PATSY: You never guess what happened to me last night –

MAGGIE: You found a cure for cancer.

PATSY: Nah, I did my first baby-sitting.

She waits for an enthusiastic response. None forthcoming.

Three quid an hour.

MAGGIE: That's great Patsy.

PATSY: This woman from our block met my mum down the newsagents, said I looked growed up enough to do it if I wanted the cash. Two little boys, Devon's six and Jamal's eight.

MAGGIE: And was it good fun?

PATSY: Jamal's got a bit of a gob on 'im but I sorted that out.

MAGGIE: Good.

PATSY: Got a bit of a confession to make though.

MAGGIE: Go on.

PATSY: Don't go mental –

PATSY fishes around in her bag and pulls out the molten remains of her plastic baby Victoria. It has obviously been set alight and is hideously blackened and contorted. MAGGIE looks up for the first time but doesn't seem at all phased.

Devon tiefed my lighter and set fire to her on the balcony.

MAGGIE: You'll have to explain to the management.

PATSY: Who's the management?

MAGGIE: Tom.

PATSY: Thought you could say something for me.

MAGGIE: Why?

PATSY: Because, well, you'd do it better innit.

MAGGIE: Patsy, you've destroyed school property. Talk to Tom.

PATSY: I didn't do nothing. I told you, it was that little shit Devon –

MAGGIE: You were responsible for that doll, yes?

PATSY: Yeah.

MAGGIE: And you signed a form saying that you'd look after it and return it in good order when we decided the time was right?

PATSY: Yeah, but –

MAGGIE takes the doll off PATSY and holds it up.

MAGGIE: Is it in good order?

PATSY: It's got a bit burnt that's all.

The doll's head falls off. It begins to cry, a horrible distorted squeal, as if it was in agony. MAGGIE drops it on her desk and gets back to her packing.

What d'you think Tom will say?

MAGGIE: I dunno. Depends what kind of mood he's in. Might say nothing, might make you pay for a replacement.

PATSY: Pay?

MAGGIE: You agreed to look after it.

PATSY: I'm not fuckin' payin' for nothin'! I didn't want it in the first place!

MAGGIE: Talk to Tom.

PATSY: If he tells me to pay, I'll shove it up his arse.

MAGGIE: Fine, you do that.

Beat. The doll is still crying. PATSY stamps on it repeatedly. Hideous gurgles and splutters until the doll finally gives up the ghost and is silent. PATSY watches MAGGIE as she continues to pack.

PATSY: What you doing then?

MAGGIE: Packing up my stuff.

PATSY: Why?

MAGGIE: I've decided to leave.

PATSY: You can't just leave.

MAGGIE: I can do whatever I want.

PATSY: What about us?

MAGGIE: What about you?

PATSY: We haven't finished writing our stories.

MAGGIE: (*Incredulous.*) So now you want to do some work?

Beat.

PATSY: Is this because of the thing with Lanny and Brendan?

MAGGIE: No. It's got nothing to do with any of you.

PATSY: You had a beef with Tom?

MAGGIE: That's my business.

PATSY: So it is Tom then –

MAGGIE: Just leave it.

PATSY: I could talk to him, tell him we'll all get on better from now on.

JAY enters the room.

MAGGIE: Morning Jay.

JAY: Morning.

PATSY: (*To JAY.*) Everything was alright before you came.

MAGGIE: Patsy –

JAY: What've I done?

PATSY: You've only been here a few days and now Maggie's leaving 'cos she's had some bust-up with Tom.

JAY: I'm sorry.

MAGGIE: You've got nothing to be sorry about. Patsy's just looking for someone to blame. There's always got to be someone to blame, right?

JAY: It's my fault.

MAGGIE: It isn't anybody's fault.

JAY: On my first day, I saw you kissing in the garden.

PATSY: Ha ha.

But PATSY stops laughing when MAGGIE's face tells her it's true.

JAY: And I called Tom's wife to tell her.

MAGGIE: (*Incredulous.*) You little snake. Why'd you do that? Why would anyone do a thing like that?

PATSY: (*Amused.*) You and Tom?

MAGGIE: I advise you to drop it Patsy –

PATSY: He's older than my Grandad –

MAGGIE: Quiet!

MAGGIE turns to JAY.

I'm sorry I called you a snake –

PATSY: Yeah, she ain't the one been shagging a married –

MAGGIE: Patsy, I swear I'll –

PATSY: Alright, alright.

MAGGIE: (*To JAY.*) I just don't understand what would make you do that.

JAY: It was a joke.

MAGGIE: Well I hope somebody's laughing.

JAY: Will they kick me out?

MAGGIE: Is that what you want?

JAY: I don't care.

MAGGIE: No, they won't kick you out Jay.

TOM pops his head round the door.

TOM: Maggie, can I have a word in my office please?

MAGGIE: Not now.

TOM: Please.

MAGGIE: Anything you've got to say you can say in here.

TOM comes inside.

TOM: Okay, in that case, Patsy, Jay, would you mind popping outside – ?

MAGGIE: No, they can stay here. Any conversations we have from now on, I want independent verification.

TOM: Independent verification?

MAGGIE: It's a legal thing apparently.

TOM edges closer to MAGGIE holding an envelope in his hand.

TOM: (*Half-whisper.*) There was no need to do this –

MAGGIE: Speak up.

TOM: (*Louder now.*) There was no need to do this –

MAGGIE: To do what?

TOM: To hand in your resignation.

MAGGIE: You threaten me with legal action, and it surprises you that I don't fancy working here anymore?

TOM: I've got the LEA due in quarter of an hour, you can't just leave us –

MAGGIE: According to my union, in the circumstances I'd be crazy not to.

Beat. TOM looks warily at the two girls. JAY hangs her head, PATSY just smiles.

TOM: What are you smiling at?

PATSY: Didn't know you had it in you.

TOM: Had what in me?

PATSY: Dirty old devil.

TOM twigs.

TOM: (*To MAGGIE.*) Oh, that's just great. So you're employing damaged kids as confidantes now? What's that about? Trying to undermine their respect for me before you fly off?

MAGGIE: I'm not the one shouting and swearing Tom.

TOM tries to calm himself.

TOM: Alright, alright, last night, I didn't mean what I said… I'd had too much to drink and it all just got out of hand.

PATSY: Ha ha.

TOM: Oh *shut* up, you stupid bitch!

PATSY: You can't call me that!

TOM: (*To MAGGIE.*) Please Maggie.

PATSY: He can't call me that…stupid old cunt!

MAGGIE: You're losing it Tom.

TOM: What?

MAGGIE: Listen to yourself. You've just called one of your students a bitch. It's a joke.

MAGGIE picks up her crate. Beat.

TOM: Okay, okay. Patsy I apologise. Now can we please just forget about all this…this horrible mess.

MAGGIE: I'll stay on one condition.

TOM: Okay –

MAGGIE: You go.

Beat.

TOM: No, I can't do that.

MAGGIE: Why not? You hate the job, you hate the kids and I imagine you're starting to hate yourself –

TOM: I'm not going anywhere.

MAGGIE: Fine. Then I will.

As MAGGIE walks toward the door, LANNY bursts through it, his face screwed into a tight ball of anger. Sensing the worst, MAGGIE puts the crate down.

Lanny?

But LANNY doesn't want her. He strides over to TOM. For a second he looks like he may hit him, but manages to rein himself in.

LANNY: I waited for you –

TOM: Okay Orlando, if you'll just let me explain –

LANNY: Six thirty at the gates you said. I waited 'til seven.

TOM: I'm sorry but I got tied up –

PATSY: Ha ha, he's been well busy –

LANNY: You promised!

LANNY kicks a desk over. JAY jumps up and moves to stand by MAGGIE.

MAGGIE: Lanny, we can put this right if you just calm down.

LANNY: How you goin' to put this right? They turned me down. The cunts turned me down. Said they were expecting a personal reference. Soon as they found out I was on my own, you could see they'd made up their minds.

MAGGIE: What did your mum say to them?

LANNY: My mum didn't fuckin' come because he said he was coming. She thought it was sorted.

TOM: I'm sorry Orlando but –

LANNY: You're sorry? I've been waiting three months for this.

MAGGIE: I'll give the school a ring now, see what they say.

LANNY: No, phone call's no good. I want him to come with me now. Explain why he let me down. I want him to tell them why he fucked my life up.

PATSY: Because he was tryin' to get in her pants innit.

MAGGIE: Is that helpful Patsy?

LANNY: I want you to come with me now.

LANNY fixes TOM hard. Beat.

Now.

TOM: (*Calmly at first, then building.*) Who do you think you are? What makes you think you can just storm in here and order me about like some playground bully?

MAGGIE: (*Warning.*) Tom –

TOM: What? D'you think I'm scared of you? You think I haven't come across kids like you before? Over and over, year after year, you all roll in the door and I have to pretend that you're all different with individual problems that need personalised solutions. Well, fuck you! Truth is, you're just a nasty little thug and one of two things'll happen to you: you'll either live a hollow existence in some crappy flat, sucking the life out of every unfortunate bastard who can't outrun you or you'll end up shot, stabbed, fucked on crack or, odds-on, banged up half your adult life –

PATSY: Lanny's gonna be a forensick thingie –

TOM: Well we can all dream, but the sad truth is Lanny's not going to be anything very much –

LANNY pulls out his knife.

LANNY: We'll see about that.

TOM applauds lazily.

TOM: Oh, nice move Orlando.

MAGGIE: (*Calming.*) Put the knife away.

LANNY: I want you to come with me now and explain.

TOM: Or else you'll what? Stab me, slash me, or what is it they say in the films… 'I'm gonna gut you like a fish'? Is that what you had in mind?

PATSY: (*Worried now.*) Why don't you just go with him?

TOM: Because I'm in charge here not him, because I don't like the way he's asking me, and because I've got two men coming round any minute who are trying their hardest to close this centre down. So I'm going to stay right here and smile and nod and convince them that they shouldn't – you're going to sit down and get on with some work and Lanny's going to give me the knife and then he's going home to calm down –

LANNY: No.

TOM: Fine. We'll all just wait here then.

Beat.

Is it okay if we sit down?

LANNY nods. TOM sits. An uneasy silence.

Wealthy bored people would probably pay lots of money for this kind of kick –

MAGGIE: Will you just shut up –

TOM: The life-affirming hostage experience.

PATSY: Who's a hostage?

TOM: We are.

LANNY: No you're not.

TOM: Okay, you're holding us in a room against our will at knife point but we're not hostages –

LANNY: No.

TOM: Fine.

BRENDAN enters the room, his face still swollen from yesterday's attack. He sees TOM.

BRENDAN: (*Sullen.*) Mary says there are two blokes to see you.

TOM: Well could you ask if they can wait until we've sorted this out.

BRENDAN: You got legs haven't you?

TOM: I'm not allowed to leave the room.

LANNY: Close the door Brendan you stupid fuck!

PATSY: Lanny's holding us all hostage.

BRENDAN sees the knife.

BRENDAN: Fuckin' A Lanny, you finally flipped!

LANNY: I'm not holding anyone hostage!

TOM: Let's look it up, might as well get some educational benefit from this – you got a dictionary in here Miss Bates?

MAGGIE: This isn't a joke Tom.

TOM takes a dictionary from the crate.

TOM: I'm not joking, and I'm pretty sure Lanny's not –

MAGGIE: You're just winding him up, d'you *want* someone to get hurt?

TOM: (*Flicking through dictionary.*) Glockenspiel… heliometer…hope…horticulture…hostage. 'A person given to or held by another against their will as a security or pledge'. We're being held aren't we? Or are we? Maybe it'd be alright if I just…left the room.

BRENDAN: Are you still drunk or what?

TOM: Probably. *Would* you stop me if I left Lanny?

TOM walks slowly toward the door, but LANNY stands in his way.

LANNY: You promised you'd come.

TOM: *Am* I a hostage?

MAGGIE: Tom, stop playing these silly little games –

TOM is only feet away from LANNY.

TOM: Am I being held against my will? If you don't tell me, I should just walk out the door.

LANNY: I just wanted you to come with me to Larkhill.

TOM: Make up your mind Lanny – am I a hostage or not?

LANNY: I told all my friends I was coming back.

TOM is within striking distance now.

TOM: See, I don't think I'm a hostage at all. I think I could just walk out that door.

LANNY: No, you gotta come with me.

LANNY points the knife at TOM's chest.

TOM: I think I could just walk out that door and get on with my day.

PATSY: He's just trying to make him angry innit.

TOM: Because *you* couldn't stop me.

BRENDAN: Maggie, *do* something.

MAGGIE: Lanny, just let him go and we'll forget all about this okay?

TOM edges closer so the knife point is resting on his chest. The others look on in horror.

TOM: See Maggie thinks you've got something about you. Thinks people like you've got this little piece of goodness still buried deep down in all that bad boy crap. And she reckons that if she waters that seed everyday, it'll start to grow…and it'll grow and grow, a warm glow flowing through your veins, the good stuff taking over your whole body, transforming you into a wonderful human being. A nice guy. A useful member of society. Me? I used to think like that too. And I watered those seeds just like Maggie. And I waited. But nothing happened. So I gave it another go, year after year, boys and girls just like you. And now it's suddenly hit me full in the face. I've wasted my life, because there is no good in a person like you. Holding a knife to my chest like some half-arsed gangster, screaming and shouting when you don't get what you want like a baby, like a fucking baby with muscles you are, a pathetic baby. Remember I talked about your sorrow? Well, I didn't mean it. You don't deserve a *thing*, because you're just a nasty, weak, stupid little boy –

LANNY drops the knife to the floor and walks away from TOM.

PATSY: You're not any of them things Lanny, don't listen to him.

TOM: Right, so now we've left gangster mode have we?

LANNY: Just leave me alone.

MAGGIE: Drop it now Tom.

Whilst the others focus on LANNY and TOM, JAY picks up LANNY's knife.

BRENDAN: Well out of order.

TOM: You don't approve? Well, I'm very sorry.

MAGGIE: Just get out now, let me to see to this.

TOM: Okay, come on then Orlando.

MAGGIE: He should stay here.

TOM: You know the rules Maggie. He's threatened to attack a member of staff.

MAGGIE: I never actually heard him make a threat.

TOM: We'll let the police sort that out.

PATSY: The police?

MAGGIE: There's no need for that.

TOM: So you think your students should be allowed to hold knives to their teacher's throats?

MAGGIE: Of course I don't, but the whole incident has to be put in context –

TOM: Am I right in thinking you resigned this morning?

MAGGIE: Yes, but –

TOM: The hostage crisis is over, so why are you still here?

MAGGIE: Maybe I should stay and help sort this out.

TOM: Orlando goes with the police, the other three can be slotted into other groups, what's to sort out?

MAGGIE: Why are you behaving like this?

TOM: Behaving like what? Now, if you'll excuse me, I've got some important visitors waiting outside. Give your keys to Mary on the way out.

TOM walks toward the door, but JAY blocks the way. She holds the knife. For a moment, TOM looks worried. A beat, then JAY carefully hands TOM the knife.

Thank you.

JAY: This isn't right…what you're doing, it isn't right –

TOM: Thank you Jay. Maggie, pack your things, Orlando, come with me. The rest of you wait here.

TOM makes for the door. LANNY follows him.

JAY: You shouldn't have hit Brendan.

TOM: Sorry?

JAY: That was your mistake. You shouldn't have hit him.

TOM: What on earth are you on about?

JAY: (*To BRENDAN.*) How did you get those bruises?

BRENDAN: (*Confused.*) You know how I got them.

JAY: Yeah. I saw it all. We all saw it.

TOM: What on earth are you on about?

JAY: You were angry, you lost your temper –

BRENDAN: You were like a tidal wave.

JAY: Like a volcano.

BRENDAN: Someone just flicked your switch and it was like – bam!

BRENDAN mimes kicking hell out of an imaginary body.

JAY: Brendan was winding you up and you just flipped.

BRENDAN: Flipped one-eighty, you crazy fuck!

TOM: You're saying I hit Brendan?

JAY: We all saw it, didn't we Lanny?

LANNY nods.

Patsy?

PATSY: Volcanger innit Lanny?

LANNY: Bigtime volcanger.

JAY: Saw the red mist falling over your eyes.

BRENDAN: Called me a cunt and kicked me in the balls.

PATSY: Kung fu and shit.

JAY: And then Brendan fell to the floor, remember?

BRENDAN: I was in agony mate, agony.

JAY: But you just wouldn't stop –

PATSY: You laid in with your boots – bam-bam-bam!

BRENDAN: I'm crying out in pain.

JAY: Jumped on Bren's chest – started punching him in the face –

LANNY: Tried to drag you off, but I was too weak, too pathetic and weak –

JAY: And Bren's face was all bloody and we were all screaming for help, for someone, anyone to help –

BRENDAN: You broke my fuckin' nose you bastard!

JAY: See we trusted you and you let us down.

PATSY: Let us down bigtime.

JAY: And that is what happened, yesterday at three in the afternoon. We all saw it.

TOM chuckles.

TOM: Priceless, just bloody priceless. Now I've just got one question to ask: where were you when all this was happening Miss Bates?

Beat. MAGGIE can't look at him.

MAGGIE: Me? I was watching you kick the shit out of Brendan.

TOM's face falls in disbelief.

I've always said to my kids that we can have secrets in here Tom. What goes on in this room stays in this room.

TOM is about to say something, but thinks better of it.

You'd better go speak to those nice men from the LEA.

BRENDAN: Don't slam the...

TOM exits, slamming the door.

ALL: Door!

The lights snap off and we hear music. The lights slowly fade back up to night-time. The moon is full, casting strange shadows of trees and vines twisting themselves up the wall. The garden is creeping into the classroom – overgrown, wild, unchecked – gradually spreading, spreading, until the stage is a mass of verdant green...

13

Paradise. We see JAY, asleep in the garden, her head resting on pillows. She wakes with a start and, like a sleepwalker roused in unfamiliar territory, checks her surroundings, looking for clues...

JAY: I'm in a garden. It's a perfect garden. Wild like a baby, like a new-born baby. In the distance, I hear children, laughing, playing...something secret hissing in the bushes...there's a me-shaped hole in the ground...and I don't know why.

LANNY and PATSY enter. PATSY's heavily pregnant.

PATSY: You know where you are girl?

JAY: Just fade away to nothing –

LANNY: This ain't no dream, you get me?

JAY: To be nothing…

BRENDAN runs on-stage, arms spread wide, pretending to be an aeroplane.

BRENDAN: We are the naughty boys, the naughty girls – naughty, naughty, naughty!

LANNY: We're the boom –

BRENDAN: The bollocks.

PATSY: Oh *yes*, we're fine.

BRENDAN: Stay and play for a while?

JAY: I think someone's calling me –

PATSY: She don't think she belongs here –

JAY: No.

PATSY: She don't think she's bad like us.

BRENDAN: Bad meaning good?

PATSY: Nah, bad meaning bad. Naturally bad.

LANNY: Deep down bad. The *original* bad.

BRENDAN: From the original sin. Can't win. We were born this way, see?

PATSY: Bitch be out of here quicktime.

LANNY: Nuff now. It ends.

But PATSY pushes JAY. JAY responds by pushing PATSY back. PATSY reaches inside her shirt and pulls out the cushion that had been masquerading as a baby – she thwacks JAY with it. JAY picks a cushion from the ground, tries to belt her back but hits LANNY. LANNY reciprocates. BRENDAN joins in, smacking LANNY, then PATSY, forcing PATSY to counter with an awesome blow to the side of BRENDAN's head that sends him reeling. The perfect garden is being destroyed, as the pillow fight continues with ever-changing allegiances, punctuated by the sound of shouts and squeals and lots of laughter. The music fades up as the children continue punching and kicking, laughing and squealing as the lights fade to black.

The End.